DRIVE IT!

The Complete Book of

FORMULA 2 MOTOR RACING

Tristan Wood

Foulis

Haynes

ISBN 0 85429 366 3

© Haynes Publishing Group

First published 1984

A FOULIS Motoring Book

Published by:
Haynes Publishing Group
Sparkford, Yeovil, Somerset BA22 7JJ

Distributed in USA by:
Haynes Publications Inc.
861 Lawrence Drive, Newbury Park, California 91320 USA

Editor: Mansur Darlington
Layout design: Barry Griffiths
Dust jacket design: Phill Jennings
Printed and bound by: J. H. Haynes & Co. Ltd.

Contents

Foreword

When one considers just how much has been written about Grand Prix racing, and that Formula 2 has been thriving as its immediate junior for virtually as long as Formula 1 has existed, it is remarkable that until now no book has been available on this most deserving subject.

After two years of contesting the European Formula 2 Championship, I have great enthusiasm and respect for the type of racing it provides. At a cost of perhaps a tenth of the equivalent Formula 1 budget, Formula 2 has many of the qualities of a Grand Prix; an international field, professional teams, three day events and above all, fiercely contested good length races.

We all tend to follow recognised names only in any sport, and this contributes to the much smaller crowds and media interest Formula 2 attracts. But perhaps to an extent this is its forté too; without all the commercial show of Grand Prix racing Formula 2 shines through as motor racing for the purist, with little to camouflage the efforts of the determined teams, engineers and drivers.

Tristan Wood has provided an excellent insight into the somewhat obscure world of Formula 2 in this book. Particularly interesting for me is the comprehensive history of the category, and it is upon absorbing this that one realises that most of the names, whether drivers, team managers or designers, are the same as those in a Grand Prix publication — they just feature a few years earlier!

It is very readable, uncomplicated and not bogged down with technical detail. All aspects are covered thoroughly; drivers, cars and races through a description of the circuits to even the method of Formula 2 administration.

In its field, Tristan Wood's book has no

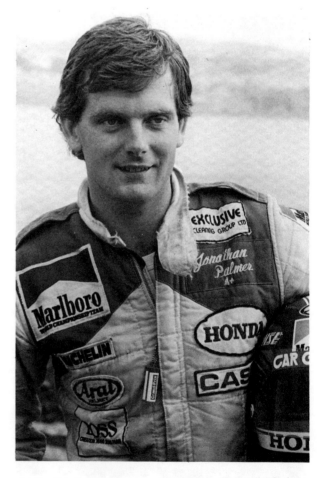

rivals, and learning more about Formula 2 is a must for anybody truly interested in the sport.

Jonathan Palmer

Introduction

"A vital stage in a young driver's development."

"Features some of the finest racing to be seen anywhere."

"Friendly, but intensely competitive – essentially, a sport with a capital S."

"Unlike Grand Prix racing, it has not become totally subservient to big-money interests".

"Forget F1 – contains more real racers than any other category."

Such are the statements which have been made about Formula 2 motor racing in recent years, when Grand Prix racing's reputation has been tarnished by frequent reports of regularity protests, organisational feuds, circuit bans, driver walkouts and dull processional races.

Caught in a blinding media spotlight and fuelled by the big-money investments of multinational companies and the like, it is inevitable in F1, to attain superiority over their rivals, that teams will continue to look to loopholes rather than follow the spirit of the regulations; that everyone pouring money into the Formula will also be striving to get as much out of it as possible; that Grand Prix venues will often be chosen more for their commercial possibilities (as epitomised by the Caesar's Palace car park at Las Vegas) than for their ability to genuinely test driver and car (Nürburgring, Montjuich, Clermont Ferrand where are you now?); and that some drivers will be competing because of their wealthy backers rather than on merit, whilst others have become somewhat jaded with the whole wearying business.

On the other hand, F2, which, despite participation by works teams, remains a customer-orientated formula, has a remarkable history of constructors keen to reach agreement on any unclear regulations so as to produce cars which are pretty equally matched, and of close racing by the world's up-and-coming young drivers on a variety of interesting and demanding circuits. With its attractive, scaled-down versions of F1 cars and increasing television coverage around the world, F2 is growing more and more popular with spectators and competitors alike. It, too, is an expensive sport (a team's season will cost in the region of £150,000 per entry) constantly faced with the difficult task of keeping costs down so that privateers can continue to take part, but this aim has been reasonably well achieved to date, despite the growing involvement of tyre and component manufacturers. For the drivers and some teams, F2 continues to be a valuable training ground for elevation to F1 racing, and for spectators, F2 has proven itself to be a heady and exciting single-seater category.

Apart from the main European series, F2 racing also takes place in other parts of the world. In Japan, the Formula has comprised the country's premier motor racing category for several years now (in 1983, the Japanese F2 Championship was contested over eight races from March to November). European drivers frequently appear in individual championship rounds, and the series has stimulated involvement in Europe by Japanese concerns like Honda and Bridgestone and racecar manufacturers like Nova. The other main marketplace for F2 chassis is South Africa, where the cars run with Mazda engines in a national series, while F2 machines of various vintage can be found in Formula Libre events all over the world, from South America to Eire.

Indeed, F2 is no modern phenomenon. Since the birth of motor sport, the concept of a category for less powerful, scaled-down versions of the premier racing cars of the day has always existed.

Believe it or not, this is the ancestor of the modern F2 racing car! A family pose beside a touring version of the Decauville Voiturelle which won the voiturette class in the 1898 Paris-Amsterdam-Paris Race.

The 1912 Sunbeam team which dominated the Coupe de l'Auto section of the French Grand Prix. Designer Louis Coatalen is flanked by the voiturettes of Medinger (52), Resta (17), Rigal (3) and Caillois (16).

Debonair Englishman Mike Hawthorn gained Ferrari's attentions by entering his Cooper-Bristol in a number of international events in 1952. Here he is on his way to third place at the British Grand Prix, Silverstone.

At the start of the century, such vehicles were known as voiturettes. Smaller and lighter than the top racing cars of the time, they nevertheless frequently competed in the same races albeit as a separate class. The first such event was the 1898 Paris-Amsterdam-Paris road race, in which the voiturette section was won by Corbière on a 479cc Decauville — the same type of car with which the latter-day French heroes Gabriel and Théry cut their racing teeth.

The formula attracted the burgeoning small manufacturer market, and between 1906 and 1910, voiturette racing received the attentions of nearly 40 constructors. The definition of a voiturette at this time varied from season to season depending on the cylinder bore, although no restrictions were made on the stroke until 1910. The main voiturette series, the Coupe de l'Auto, was regarded with such importance that it was sometimes run concurrently with the French Grand Prix — the premier race of the time. By modern standards, the voiturettes were quite powerful, but Grand Prix machines in those days were often over 7 litres: that there was often little to choose between the formulas can be judged by the results of the 1912 French Grand Prix, when the Coupe de l'Auto-winning Sunbeams of Rigal, Resta and Caillois finished third, fourth and fifth overall. With a top speed of over 90mph, the scuttle-shaped British cars went on to achieve over 30 class and world records in two-seat and single-seater form.

Following the First World War, voiturette racing resumed in 1920 with a 1400cc limit, extended to 1500cc from 1921–26, at which point the same limit was imposed for Grand Prix events: the category was dominated by 4-cylinder Talbot-Darracqs in the hands of such drivers as Albert Divo, Algernon and Kenelm Lee Guiness and Henry Segrave.

Voiturettes enjoyed a popular revival in the 1930s, when the German Auto Union and Mercedes-Benz teams gained a stranglehold on Grand Prix racing. The lesser formula became an Anglo-Italian battleground, the nimble ERAs up against the compact Maserati 4C and 6CM models, the races featuring classic duels between such drivers as Mays, Seaman, Fairfield, Bira, Howe, Dobson, Peter Whitehead, Farina, Taruffi, Villoresi, Trossi, de Graffenreid, Dreyfus and Cortese. In 1936, wealthy Englishman Dick Seaman campaigned a modified and lightened 1927 Grand Prix Delage in the category, thrashing the opposition and bringing himself to the attention of Mercedes-Benz, with whom he was offered a Grand Prix seat from 1937. Towards the end of this period, Alfa Romeo produced the 158 'Alfetta', with which Guiseppe Farina (later to become motor racing's first World Champion) won a number of Italian events and the 1939

Alberto Ascari and Ferrari dominated F2 in 1952 and 1953, when the category was employed to determine the Drivers' World Championship.

Graham Hill's Lotus heads the Coopers of Salvadori and Lewis-Evans at the start of the 1958 Lavant Cup Race at Goodwood. Both marques' efforts in F2 were to lead to their adopting a radical approach to Grand Prix car design.

An unknown Jochen Rindt keeps Graham Hill at bay during the Austrian's famous drive at Crystal Palace, Whit Monday 1964.

The Brabham-Hondas of Jack Brabham and Denny Hulme swept the board in F2 in 1966.

international race at Berne.

When motor racing was re-organised after the Second World War, the Grand Prix category was referred to as Formula 1, whilst voiturette racing initially retained its original name of 'Formula B' before becoming Formula 2. The limited availability of cars dictated the Formula encompass unsupercharged cars of up to 2000cc or supercharged machines of up to 1100cc, and the category again proved popular as a less expensive form of racing than F1.

British drivers Stirling Moss (Cooper-Alta) and Peter Collins (HWM) gained their first experiences of Continental circuits in F2, competing against the French Simca-Gordinis, German BMW-powered AFMs, and Italian Maseratis and Ferraris.

In 1952, Ferrari's dominance of F1 was so unchallenged that it was decided to run the World Championship to F2 regulations for a couple of years. Although the size of Grand Prix fields increased — with works participation from Maserati, Osca, Gordini, Cooper, HWM and Connaught — the results remained the same, the squat Ferrari 500 winning virtually every race in the hands of Ascari, Villoresi, Farini, Taruffi or Hawthorn (who'd earlier made his mark in F2 at the wheel of a Cooper-Bristol). The chubby Alberto Ascari became World Champion in both years, managing 12 victories in 1952 and seven in 1953, when the Maseratis of Fangio and Gonzalez provided sterner opposition. From 1954, a new 2½-litre F1 came into being, making 2-litre F2 virtually redundant.

Three years later however, a new F2 was drawn up for unsupercharged 1500cc single-seaters, and this category paved the way to international success for the inexpensive and lightweight designs of British constructors Cooper and Lotus. Both companies put their F2 experiences to good use in their revolutionary entries into F1, the World Championship-winning rear-engined Cooper T41 and the mid-engined Lotus 18 being direct derivatives of F2 machinery. Their drivers too (Brabham, McLaren, Salvadori, Brooks, Lewis-Evans, Ireland, Graham Hill, Halford and Allison), all learnt their skills in F2 before embarking on the Grand Prix trail. By 1960, foreign firms were also making a point of using F2 as a proving ground for both cars and drivers (particularly as F1 was to be reduced to the same 1½-litres limit from 1961), and the last year of the 1500cc Formula witnessed some splendid dicing between the Lotuses of Clark and Ireland, the Ferrari of von Trips, the Porsches of Bonnier, Graham Hill and Moss and the Coopers of McLaren, Maggs and Surtees: the season ended with the F2 Constructors' Championship shared between Cooper (the 1959 champions) and Porsche, who were thereby encouraged to compete in F1 the following year, when F2 again ceased to exist.

With the only single-seater category apart from F1 being Formula Junior, the situation from 1961 proved particularly frustrating for aspiring Grand Prix competitors as there was a substantial gap in professionalism and standard of racecraft between the two formulas. And so from 1964, the existing structure of F1, F2 and F3 was established, the last two categories adopting the Formula Junior principle of production-based engines in small-scale Grand Prix-type cars.

As F1 was to remain limited to 1½ litres until 1966, F2 had to be restricted to 1000cc, but the Formula was well-supported and the Grand Prix stars of the day — Clark, Hill, Surtees, Brabham etc. — would happily mix it with up-and-coming drivers out to show their true talents against the established stars. The most outstanding 'find' was Jochen Rindt, a virtually unknown Austrian who catapulted to fame over the 1964 Whit weekend, which culminated in his achieving an astounding victory over Hill and Clark at Crystal Palace. The last year of the Formula was dominated by the neat Brabham-Hondas of Jack Brabham and Denny Hulme, this combination winning 12 of the season's 15 races from the Cosworth-powered opposition.

For 1967, when the Formula was altered to allow production engines of 1300–1600cc, the FIA also decided to institute a Drivers' European Championship (a similar championship, covering Grand Prix events and determined by committee, had run from 1935–39, and was won by Caracciola on three occasions and by Rosemeyer and Lang once). With regular Grand Prix contenders unable to compete for championship honours, the Formula was set on a course in which it would identify the most promising young drivers of the day and help prepare them for future Grand Prix careers. Over the subsequent 17 years, the Formula has continued to prosper on such a basis, and, from being a relaxed opportunity for F1 stars to do battle with 'unknowns' in equally-matched and inexpensive machinery, has progressed to the highly professional and keenly-fought series for the young pretenders that it is today.

Whether you're a spectating enthusiast or would-be competitor, this book aims to give you the whys, wherefores and background of F2 racing — one of the most competitive motor sport spectacles in the world.

1 The History

With the decision made as early as 1964 to alter F2 to a 1½-litre stockblock formula, a great deal of chassis and engine development took place to ensure healthy entries right from the start of the Formula three years later. Cosworth produced a run of forty 200bhp four-valve engines (FVAs), designed around the Ford Cortina cylinder block and retailing at £2,500 each, and quickly sold all of them to the works Brabham, Cooper, Lotus, Lola, McLaren and Matra teams and a number of the better-off privateers. Lola hedged their bets, agreeing to supply their T100 chassis to BMW in return for an option to use the German company's radial four-valve Apfelbeck engine, rumoured to be a match for the Cosworth. Ferrari, too, were working hard on race preparing a Dino V6 engine in production by Fiat.

A crowded calendar of no less than 24 races indicated the enthusiasm with which race organisers greeted the new Formula. Apart from Grands Prix and the classic sports car races, F2 represented their only opportunity to feature the F1 stars the paying public flocked to see, and in these pre-recession days a F2 field featuring the likes of Brabham, Clark, Hill, Surtees, McLaren, Stewart and Rindt amounted to a strong crowd puller.

However, the introduction of the European Racing Trophy for non-graded drivers was not such a popular move. Indeed, the French organisers, desiring small-size fields packed with Grand Prix drivers rather than larger entries of unknown hopefuls, decided to have nothing to do with the new championship and arranged a four-race Trophées de France series with selected entries and its own team competition. Britain also contributed to the championship confusion, running three European Championship rounds as well as two other events, all of which comprised a series for an open RAC British Racing Car Championship and a further championship run by *Autocar* for which only British and Commonwealth drivers were eligible. While the European Championship was spread across ten races in England, Germany, Austria, Spain, Holland and Italy, there was a small number of other one-off races as well which weren't concerned with any championship at all.

Nevertheless, all the works teams took the new championship seriously enough to back non-graded runners. The factory Brabham BT23s were piloted by Brabham and Hulme once more but had the wily Australian Frank Gardner as a third works entry. Jochen Rindt headed the Winkelmann Racing Team's Brabham entries, with team-mate Alan Rees a major championship contender. Former F3 drivers Chris Lambert and Robin Widdows headed the privateer Brabham teams.

Matra Sports fielded two non-graded drivers in Jean-Pierre Beltoise and Johnny Servoz-Gavin, while the promising Belgian, Jacky Ickx, supported the graded Jackie Stewart in Ken Tyrell's Matra International set-up. The French veteran (but non-graded) Jo Schlesser raced an MS5 with support from Ford France. Lola fielded John Surtees and the non-graded Chris Irwin. Lotus and McLaren split their graded and non-graded efforts: Clark, Hill and McLaren driving works cars, while Lotus Components fielded Jackie Oliver and John Coombs was entrusted with a McLaren for Piers Courage.

Coopers had to rely totally on non-graded drivers (Beckwith, Cardwell, Rollinson and Gethin among others) to restore their racing fortunes, while Ron Harris entered the Formula's most unusual car, the Frank Costin designed wooden

Protos, for Brian Hart and young motorcyclist Eric Offenstadt. The BMW challenge consisted of the graded Jo Siffert and the ungraded Hubert Hahne, while the Ferrari project featured Jonathan Williams, a promising Englishman who had raced in Italy for some years.

True to expectations, these small, similarly-engined cars produced some incredibly close and exciting racing right from the start of the season, when Rindt's Brabham beat Hill's Lotus by a nose after a race-long dice at the Formula's first event at Snetterton. Despite the close racing (aided by fixtures at dangerous slipstreaming circuits like Hockenheim, Rheims and Enna), 1967 was the year in which Jochen Rindt was proclaimed F2 King, the brilliant Austrian winning nine, and coming second in four, of the 15 races he contested, taking the British Championship and helping Winkelmann Racing to the Trophées de France title. Always a front runner, Rindt impressed particularly at Pau, the Nürburgring and Brands Hatch, where the Winkelmann Brabham led unchallenged from start to finish.

Clark and Surtees (who, at a rain-drenched Mallory Park, finished 3½ laps up on the second-placed car) were other graded drivers to score F2 victories, but Rindt's chief rival was Jackie Stewart. The Scot had a poor finishing record in the Tyrell Matra MS5, but, once armed with the sturdier MS7, Stewart challenged Clark strongly at the new Jarama circuit near Madrid, beat Clark and Rindt fair and square in a race-long duel at Karlskoga's Swedish Grand Prix and got the better of Rindt again at another exciting race at Albi near the season's end.

Jacky Ickx, Stewart's young team mate, took the motor racing world by storm with his performances. In the first half of the season, the European Championship was disputed between Gardner (Brabham) and Rees (Winkelmann Brabham); Ickx finished behind these two at Silverstone and promised more with a strong third place behind Rindt and Surtees at the April Eifelrennen held on the snow-lined South Circuit of the Nürburgring. The following month, in equally atrocious weather conditions at Mallory Park, Ickx's determined driving (interrupted by no less than four spins!!) was the talking point of the non-championship meeting, his Matra finally finishing fourth.

A few weekends later, Ickx chalked up his first F2 win at the non-championship Crystal Palace round, passing Bruce McLaren at half distance to score a convincing victory on the tiny London track. Then, over the summer, the 22-year-old pressed his claim to the championship title with a start-to-finish win at Zandvoort (where the organisers refused to accept any graded entries and Brighton hotelier Ian Raby crashed badly, succumbing to his injuries some months later) and a third place in a Matra 1-5 result on the ultra fast Enna circuit in Sicily. Going into the last championship round at Vallelunga in October, Ickx had a 5-point lead over Frank Gardner, the Australian needing to finish first or second in front of the impressive Belgian in order to take the title. In the event, clutch trouble prevented the Brabham driver from mounting much of a challenge, but Ickx put his seal on the championship's first year by setting fastest lap and

The first European Championship race. Hill (Lotus) leads Rindt and Rees (Winkelmann Brabhams), Stewart (Tyrell Matra), Brabham and Hulme (Brabhams) and the rest at Snetterton.

leading the two-heat affair throughout.

By this time, Ickx had already made his F1 debut for Cooper-Maserati at Monza. The drive which had undoubtedly set him on this meteoric course had occurred at the German Grand Prix in August, when 12 F2 cars were used to bolster up a thin F1 grid on the 14-mile Nürburgring course.

Ickx caused a sensation in practice, when he powered his dark green MS5 round the legendary circuit a full 20 seconds faster than Oliver in the next F2 car – a time which remained third fastest overall and would have put the tiny Matra on the front row of the grid alongside the F1 cars of Clark, Hulme and Stewart if the F1 and F2 machines had not been formed up in separate grids for their simultaneous races. The performance was maintained during the Grand Prix itself, the Matra starting 18th and Ickx moving it up to fourth by half distance, ahead of such F1 luminaries as Surtees (Honda), Amon (Ferrari),

Graham Hill (Lotus) and Rodriguez (Cooper-Maserati), and establishing a new outright circuit record until Gurney's Eagle-Westlake went faster later in the race. Ickx's unforgettable drive ended three laps from home when a front suspension ball-joint fractured, leaving Oliver to take the F2 honours in his Lotus, which had been a long way behind the Tyrell Matra.

Of the remainder of the F2 brigade, Beltoise did well to come back from two nasty crashes at Jarama and Rouen to score a number of consistent placings in his works Matra and finish third in the championship, while Piers Courage pipped *Autocar* Champion Alan Rees for fourth after a similar year, his accidents occurring at Pau and Brands Hatch. Brian Hart managed some notable drives in the cigar-shaped Protos, as did Peter Gethin in the uncompetitive Cooper. On the engine front the Cosworth FVA ruled virtually unchallenged, the BMW Apfelbeck lacking power

Jacky Ickx (Tyrell Matra-Cosworth MS5) ahead of one of the F1 Cooper-Maseratis during his astonishing drive at the German Grand Prix.

Jochen Rindt (Winkelmann Brabham-Cosworth BT23C) scrapping with Jean-Pierre Beltoise (Matra-Cosworth MS7) at Jarama in 1968: for once, the Austrian had to content himself with second place.

and reliability and the Ferrari Dino appearing just once at Rouen, the car retiring with engine problems after only seven laps.

1968 – Pour La Gloire de La France

The following year saw a reduction in the number of graded drivers appearing regularly in F2, several giving priority to an increasingly busy F1 schedule and also to the more lucrative CanAm sportscar series. The physical and financial risks involved for them in competing in F2 were demonstrated all too clearly by two incidents early in the season.

The first occurred with devastating impact on the motor racing world, when Jim Clark was killed during the first championship round at Hockenheim. On a grey and wet April day, the twice World Champion was driving in a lonely ninth place when his Lotus inexplicably swerved off one of the circuit's straights at 140mph into the thick pine forest lining the track: Clark was flung out, dying instantly from severe head injuries, and suddenly motor racing had lost one of its greatest exponents.

The second incident took place at Jarama later in the month. Jackie Stewart – who'd dominated earlier non-championship events at Montjuich (Barcelona) and Pau – grabbed pole position on the twisty Spanish circuit only to crash his Tyrell Matra in the final practice session, his car ending up among the wire fencing on the outside of the track. In his attempts to control the vehicle, Stewart badly sprained a ligament in his left wrist – an injury which persisted for several months, caused him to miss two Grands Prix and badly affected his chances for the F1 World Championship.

In the face of such deterrents, the only graded driver to compete regularly in F2 was Jochen Rindt, who achieved six victories in the Winkelmann Racing Brabham BT23C. Although less successful than in 1967 (the BT23C suffering more reliability problems than its predecessor), the Austrian was no less dominant in his mastery of the Formula. At the championship round at the BARC's new circuit at Thruxton, he put on an astonishing display, winning his heat easily and, after a poor start, charging to the front in the final and establishing a clear lead over Courage (Frank Williams Brabham) and Beltoise (Matra). At half-distance, Rindt made a rare mistake and lost control of his car at the chicane. The dark green Brabham spun, leaving the circuit backwards through an advertisement hoarding and into a ditch. Hardly had this surprising development registered with spectators when the Brabham, covered in dust and sporting a bent exhaust pipe, reappeared through the hole in the hoarding, Jochen having coolly kept the engine running and throttled his way back onto the road, still in the lead! Although now immediately in front of the battle for second place, Rindt regained his concentration, established a clear lead once more and set fastest lap on his way to victory.

The F2 King's mastery of the fast slip-streaming circuits on the calendar was evident too, Rindt taking finely-judged wins on the final lap at both the June Hockenheim and Enna meetings.

Throughout the year, drivers expressed concern at such fixtures. Even in the aftermath of Clark's accident, Hockenheim's long straights remained without safety barriers and drivers were concerned that any mistake in the middle of a slipstreaming pack could provoke a terrible pile-up.

Their fears were confirmed at the non-championship Monza Lotteria race, which featured no graded drivers as it clashed with the Dutch Grand Prix. Seventeen of the 22 contestants grouped themselves together in the leading bunch, until Derek Bell's Ferrari spun in the middle of the pack on the fast Parabolica curve. Vic Elford's Brabham ricocheted off the car, triggering an alarming series of high-speed accidents within the space of a second. The Ferraris of Bell, Brambilla and Baghetti all ended up in the catchfencing where they were joined by the Brabhams of Elford, Ahrens and Westbury, but the worst hit was Jean-Pierre Jaussaud, whose Tecno shot into the air, rolled over and landed in a fiery heap: the Frenchman was flung out and suffered broken legs and ribs. Despite this incident, the race ended in good humour with a close-fought duel between the Brabhams of Rees and Jonathan Williams (deputising for Piers Courage) and the McLarens of Schlesser and Widdows. The Winkelmann driver attempted to out-psyche his opponents by waving his fist in the air as they drew alongside, only to be met by two fingers from Jo Schlesser! The race, however, went to Williams by 0.2 seconds. Monza turned out to be the last of a number of determined F2 drives by Schlesser, as the popular Frenchman was killed driving the V8 F1 Honda in his home Grand Prix: his team mate Guy Ligier immediately put the Ecurie InterSports McLarens up for sale, retiring from race driving himself, only to emerge some years later as a racing car constructor.

1968 was a tragic year for motor racing, and yet another fatality occurred, at the Zandvoort championship meeting in July, when Clay Regazzoni, storming through the field after his Tecno's engine had died on the opening lap, tangled with the Brabham of promising privateer Chris Lambert at West Tunnel. The Tecno somersaulted without harm to the Swiss, but the Brabham careered off the track, down a bank and onto the subway road, killing Lambert instantly. A number of allegations of dangerous driving were made — particularly by Lambert's father — but Regazzoni was later officially absolved from any blame for his part in the crash.

It was at this race that the European Championship was clinched by Jean-Pierre Beltoise in a works Matra MS7. This all-French combination dominated the nine-race series: Zandvoort was the sixth championship round, and Beltoise had already claimed maximum points in each round he'd started, winning at Hockenheim and Jarama and finishing second to Rindt at Thruxton and Langenlebarn. The Dutch race marked the Frenchman's third outright victory. The most impressive of these had been at Jarama in April, Rindt and Beltoise going away into a clear lead after a startline contretemps delayed the rest of the field, and then dicing for first place for half of the 60-lap race. Jean-Pierre got his Matra crossed up early on, ceding three seconds to the Austrian, but once recovered from this setback, he began closing on the Brabham once more, taking the lead in front of the pits on lap 22. Rindt hung on to the Matra's tail and retook the lead on the next lap, only to be demoted himself on the following circuit, driving the Brabham hard now in his efforts to keep up with his challenger. Four laps later, Rindt was in front again, but shortly afterwards Beltoise claimed the lead once more, and this time there was no stopping the Frenchman, Rindt sending some of the circuit's numerous marker cones up in the air before he eased off and settled for second place. Beltoise's other victories were won in Rindt's absence, but no one could deny him an outstanding year, culminating in France's most important championship win — one which was to ensure healthy participation in F2 by the French for years to come.

Beltoise's team mate, the bearded Henri Pescarolo, also played a significant role in Matra's domination of the championship, protecting his team leader at Hockenheim, Langenlebarn and Zandvoort and claiming runner-up position in the championship with a second place at the October Hockenheim meeting. Later that month, Pescarolo scored his first F2 win after a typically steady drive in the final Trophées de France round at Albi.

Capping Matra's year, Jackie Stewart returned to F2 racing in time to win the previous Trophées de France round at Rheims and claim the French Championship for the Ken Tyrell Matra International team.

In the face of this Matra supremacy, other championship contenders remained rather in the shade. Brabham privateers Piers Courage (fresh from a giant-killing Tasman series in his 1967 McLaren), Kurt Ahrens and Derek Bell managed some strong finishes at the start of the season, but their BT23Cs lacked reliability. Chris Irwin took his works Lola-Cosworth to a victory at the non-championship Nürburgring Eifelrennen, but his season was terminated in May when he was badly injured in a sportscar crash at the same circuit. Lola chassis were again used by BMW, who replaced their Apfelbeck engine with a lighter and simpler four-valve unit, only for Siffert and Hahne to suffer from handling problems in the few races they entered. The Bologna kart firm, Tecno, made their first foray into F2 racing — the Ron Harris team using their chassis too — and managed a number of good finishes (Regazzoni taking third in a works car at Crystal Palace, and Dickie Attwood managing the same for Ron Harris at Zandvoort) without ever becoming a real threat. The McLarens (this time entrusted to Chequered Flag Racing) and Merlyns (run by Bob Gerard) failed to shine, and the Chevron disappeared in mid-season, Frank Lythgoe Racing preferring to run Peter Gethin in a Brabham BT23C instead. The

Everything came good for Ferrari at the end of the season, Ernesto 'Tino' Brambilla taking the Dino 166 to two victories at Hockenheim and Vallelunga.

Yorkshireman finished the year in magnificent form with two outstanding drives at Albi, when exhaustion saw him spin away his lead to racewinner Pescarolo, and Vallelunga, where he finished third overall after splitting the Ferraris for second in the final heat.

After an indifferent F2 attempt the previous year, Ferrari launched a major challenge in 1968, beginning the season with their F1 drivers, Amon and Ickx, at the wheels of their Dino 166s but lacking a non-graded driver to go for the championship. Brian Redman, following some promising performances in the David Bridges Lola, was given a trial drive at the Nürburgring Eifelrennen, the Lancastrian making a notable impression when he continually lowered the lap record after he had come into the pits with a badly bruised eye from a stone shattering his goggles, resuming with Ickx's tinted night goggles to finish fourth. Unfortunately, a broken arm at the Belgian Grand Prix put him out for the rest of the season and so the partnership was discontinued.

Ferrari's first F2 win was narrowly missed in May when Jacky Ickx, in front of his home crowd at Zolder, deprived Chris Amon of a heat win which would have given the New Zealander overall victory. By the summer, Ferrari had signed

Derek Bell and entered him alongside Italians Ernesto 'Tino' Brambilla, Mario Casoni and veteran Giancarlo Baghetti for a four-car attack on the Monza Lotteria: the Englishman's spin triggered the multiple accident which removed three of the Ferraris on the spot.

In the end, it was Ernesto Brambilla who most rose to the occasion of a Ferrari drive. After hairy but impressive showings in his own Brabham BT23 at Langenlebarn and Enna, Brambilla returned to the Ferrari fold for the last two championship rounds at Hockenheim and Vallelunga. Armed with the latest Firestone tyres, the Italian kept up front throughout the German race, wildly passing Pescarolo on the grass on the last lap to snatch Ferrari's first win of the Formula. At Vallelunga, 'Tino' put on a much more mature and smooth performance to win both heats and overall victory from team mate Andrea de Adamich (returning to racing following his shunt in practice for the F1 Race of Champions at the start of the year), both drivers being mobbed by their compatriots at the end.

These results were good enough for Brambilla to take third place in the championship, and really put Ferrari on the F2 map. In the winter Argentine Temporada series, the Dinos confirmed

Jacky Ickx, guest-driving in Alistair Walker's Brabham-Cosworth BT23C, breathes down the neck of Jochen Rindt (Winkelmann Lotus-Cosworth 59B) at Zolder.

Jackie Stewart (Coombs Matra-Cosworth MS7) leads Rindt on the Langenlebarn airfield: once again, the Austrian emerged victorious.

they were now the cars to beat, Brambilla and de Adamich finishing 1–2 at the opening race in Buenos Aires, and de Adamich going on to chalk up two wins and a fifth race in the remaining three races to become overall Temporada victor; Ferrari now looked set to dominate F2.

1969 – Three in a Row

But it was not to be. By the time the European season began again at Thruxton in April, Cosworth had revised their FVA engine to produce 230 bhp and the three-valve Italian engines were effectively outclassed. For Ferrari drivers Brambilla, Derek Bell and Clay Regazonni, 1969 proved to be a severe disappointment.

Armed with the Cosworth 'Series 9' FVAs, Brabham produced a new spaceframe BT30 chassis, which suffered from production delays but eventually found its way to privateers Piers Courage (Frank Williams Racing), Kurt Ahrens and Peter Westbury among others. Piers – by now a graded driver – came from behind on the last corner in both heats on the slipstreaming Enna circuit to score his first F2 win at the penultimate championship round. He received no less than five cups and a gold medal for his efforts!

The faithful old BT23C continued to do well also, Brian Hart and Robin Widdows claiming wins for Bob Gerard Racing at non-championship events at Hockenheim and Monza. 250cc motorcycle champion Bill Ivy caused a sensation when, at Thruxton, he shared the front row of the grid with Rindt, Hill and Stewart on his F2 debut. The Cockney held on to fifth in the final until a rod entered the engine 12 laps from home. Ivy went on to confirm his exceptional talent, proving impressive but accident-prone at Pau and the Nürburgring, but taking a smooth fourth place at Zolder and leading at the June Hockenheim

meeting before retiring with a broken gear selection rod. This was Ivy's last F2 appearance, for he was still competing in a number of motorcycle races during his initial four-wheel season, and a practice accident on his 350cc Jawa bike at Sachsenring, East Germany, claimed his life at the beginning of July.

Another driver to shine in the BT23C was Jacky Ickx, the former European Champion guest-driving Alistair Walker's maroon example at Zolder and Rheims. At the French circuit, the Brabham took fastest practice time and led until its retirement with loss of oil, while at Zolder the Belgian again put on a magnificent display in front of his home crowd, dicing with Jochen Rindt for the lead in both heats and setting fastest lap, but having to settle for second behind the Austrian after his engine developed a misfire.

Predictably, Rindt was again the dominant force in F2, although this time in a Lotus. Having joined the Hethel company for F1, Jochen insisted he be provided with a competitive car for his favourite formula, and so Dave Baldwin produced the shark-nosed 59B to replace the out-dated Lotus 48. The Austrian won four of his eight starts, coming third once and not finishing the remainder.

Even in the hands of the experienced Winkelmann Racing set-up, the 59B suffered teething problems, and Rindt had to claw his way up from 18th grid place, following a puncture in the qualifying heat, to notch up his Easter Thruxton victory: driving without the benefit of a rev counter, he was up to second place within ten laps and through into the lead after 19, dominating the remainder of the race and setting fastest lap in a car which had only been completed two days beforehand! Pau saw a typical start-to-finish win, but, at Zolder, Rindt had to overcome

European Champion Johnny Servoz-Gavin (Coombs Matra-Cosworth MS7) on the grid at Enna alongside race winner Piers Courage (Williams Brabham-Cosworth BT30).

Ickx's persistent efforts to get by, and he enjoyed a similarly memorable dice with Jackie Stewart at Langenlebarn, the two finishing alongside each other at the end of the second heat, but overall victory eluding the Matra driver. At Albi, Rindt fell away from the front of the field with poorly bedded-in brakes, leaving eventual victory to his team mate, Graham Hill, but establishing fastest lap and helping Winkelmann to their second Trophées de France title.

Matra remained the other main contenders for outright victories, retaining the trusty MS7 with its excellent roadholding and wind-cheating characteristics. Stewart enjoyed a more extensive season in his John Coombs-managed car than he had managed in 1968, scoring two outright wins at Jarama and the Nürburgring.

The non-graded battle for the European Championship was fought between the Matras of Henri Pescarolo and Johnny Servoz-Gavin and the new Len Terry-designed BMW 269 of Hubert Hahne, and continued throughout the seven-race series.

Carrying on from where he had left off the previous season, Henri Pescarolo claimed maximum points at Thruxton, the opening round, finishing fourth overall with Servoz-Gavin classified fifth behind him (Matras occupying the four runner-up places behind Rindt's Lotus). The BMW team, however, made a special effort for the

next two rounds on their home ground, Hahne finishing second to Beltoise at Hockenheim after Pescarolo had made the wrong choice of tyre, and taking maximum points again with a fourth overall at the Eifelrennen. By the latter race, Pescarolo's championship hopes had been severely dashed by a practice accident at Le Mans which hospitalized him with burns and a broken leg.

At Jarama, the Matras proved ideally suited to the circuit once more and Stewart and Beltoise finished first and second. Hahne (driving the old Lola-chassised BMW) and Servoz-Gavin got away fifth and sixth, but the Matra was T-boned by Cevert's Tecno on the opening lap and resumed in 11th place. Thereafter, Servoz-Gavin pulled out all the stops, closing on his championship rival and attacking the BMW lap after lap until the Tyrell car got past just after half-distance, going on to take maximum points with a fourth place overall. Hahne fended off the attentions of Brambilla's Ferrari by 0.6 seconds to finish behind the Frenchman and preserve a two-point lead in the championship table.

When the championship duel resumed two months later at the airfield circuit of Langenlebarn, John Coombs reported that it seemed Matra wanted Pescarolo to take the honours as they had deemed that Servoz-Gavin should drive a sportscar for them in America rather than contest the Austrian round. Pescarolo, however, appeared far from recovered from his Le Mans crash and looked relieved to retire with a broken piston early on, Hahne finishing seventh overall in the streamlined BMW to earn himself four more points.

As the F2 circus arrived at Enna in August, there were rumours that the last two championship races, scheduled for Vallelunga and Syracuse, would be cancelled due to the organisers finding themselves in financial difficulties. With drivers complaining that too many cars were allowed out on the Sicilian slipstreaming track at any one time, practice saw a number of accidents. The BMW drivers experienced front suspension problems and steering wander, and the unfortunate Hahne suddenly found his car oversteering in the middle of a fast bend, the BMW leaving the track and burying its nose under a badly-positioned guardrail; the German was out of the race with a broken bone in his foot. With Pescarolo suffering a broken fuel pump in the first heat, Servoz-Gavin chalked up a heat second and fifth to be classified second overall behind Courage and go into the lead of the championship by three points from Hahne, these two now the only contenders for the title.

Following last-minute safety measures to the Vallelunga circuit, the Rome Grand Prix in October marked the final championship round. A recovered Hubert Hahne set the pace at the start of practice until Servoz-Gavin claimed pole, his Tyrell mechanics having changed the Matra's gear ratios and adopted a new Dunlop tyre compound. Unable to improve upon his times during the second day's practice, the BMW driver started sixth on the grid, and was involved in a four-car dice for fifth when, on lap 11, he spun the car in the middle of a fast right-hander, Hahne's championship hopes ending crumpled up beside a guardrail. In the meantime, Servoz-Gavin was duelling with Piers Courage for the lead, the Frank Williams team running the tiny De Tomaso on this occasion. The Italian car got by into the lead, only for Piers to lose it in his cramped cockpit conditions and drop behind: a few laps later, suffering from fatigue, Piers spun once more, this time resuming in fourth. Young Servoz-Gavin motored on to score an easy heat win, and led impressively throughout the second heat to score an overall race win and underline his championship victory. By this time, the promising Frenchman had already made his Grand Prix début for Tyrell in the Canadian Grand Prix, when, driving the four-wheel-drive Matra, Servoz-Gavin had struggled home sixth for his first World Championship point.

Of the remaining Grand Prix hopefuls in F2, François Cevert and Ronnie Peterson impressed in Tecnos, the Frenchman claiming a surprise win at the Rheims slipstreamer, while the Swede led his first F2 race at Monza before pitting with a deflating tyre. Rolf Stommelen's début single-seater drive in the F2 section of the German Grand Prix was good enough to warrant F1 team managers considering him for 1970, while at Thruxton a young Ulsterman named John Watson made his mark by holding down fifth place (leading non-graded driver) at one time until destroying his Team Ireland Lotus 48 at the Cobb-Segrave-Campbell complex, thereby terminating his F2 season.

1970 – Down To The Wire

With bag fuel tanks made mandatory for the 1970 F2 season, the MS7 was no longer eligible, and Matra decided to end their F2 interest and concentrate on sportscar and F1 racing. After their disappointments the previous year, Ferrari also preferred to cease their F2 involvement, while Lola, McLaren and Merlyn decided to throw in the towel as well.

By now, the average F2 set-up for chassis, two engines and spares was costing £7-9,000 before taking into account transportation, wages, breakages and running costs, and with several of the races originally arranged for 1969 failing to take place, there was a fear that F2 would not remain a suitable formula for investment. However, 1970 proved to be a memorable F2 season, featuring 20 races in all (compared to 1969's 15) and the, by now, habitual close racing, involving many new names and some new constructors too.

The most acclaimed of these was March, whose all-purpose F2/3/B/F space-frame was provided with bulky side-tanks and a nine-series FVA engine and which was entered by ex-privateer Malcolm Guthrie for Ronnie Peterson and the graded Chris Amon (prepared to do 'sensible circuits' only). With his works March deal falling through, Peterson's arch home-rival Reine Wisell motivated Chevron to adapt their FB car for F2 use, while the Irish firm Crosslé also produced a F2 car, albeit mainly for Formula Libre use.

Brabham returned to the forefront of the category with a modified BT30 which complied with the bag tank regulations and was raced by Jack Brabham, Jackie Stewart, Jo Bonnier (John Coombs); Henri Pescarolo, Brian Hart (Bob Gerard); Derek Bell (Wheatcroft Racing); Tino Brambilla, Robin Widdows, Alan Rollinson, Carlos Reutemann, Vittorio Brambilla, Andrea de Adamich and Peter Gethin amongst others. Lotus produced the clean, aerodynamic 69 model for Jochen Rindt Racing (Jochen Rindt and Graham Hill) and for Lotus Components, running British F3 Champion Emerson Fittipaldi for non-graded

22   With the Lotus 69 produced at his request, Jochen Rindt again dominated F2.

honours. In Matra's absence, Pygmée kept the French flag flying, with an Elf-sponsored monocoque for home talents Beltoise, Jabouille, Depailler and Dal Bo, while the Tecno team this year comprised Clay Regazzoni and François Cevert with FVAs developed by Tecno themselves. BMW also looked strong, with Jo Siffert, Jacky Ickx, Hubert Hahne, Kurt Ahrens and Dieter Quester on their driver roster.

1970 was, of course, the year Jochen Rindt took the F1 World Championship honours despite his tragic death at Monza during practice for the Italian Grand Prix. The great Austrian's F2 season suffered both from his understandable pre-occupation with the F1 title and also from his distress following the death of his friend, Piers Courage, at Zandvoort (Frank Williams and De Tomaso having combined efforts for a F1 programme this year).

Nevertheless, Rindt continued to dominate the Formula. The season began with his third consecutive win at Thruxton, and he took similarly easy victories at non-championship meetings at the Nürburgring and Zolder as well. At the Pau street circuit, he managed a further win once Jack Brabham had retired his Goodyear-shod Coombs Brabham after 19 laps in the lead, while on his last F2 appearance at the Salzburgring, Jochen's Lotus 69 retired with engine problems in the first heat but returned with a new engine to win the second heat and set fastest lap of the day. Rindt's death the following weekend stunned the motor racing world, in particular F2 enthusiasts, for many of whom Jochen simply was F2.

The European Championship for non-graded drivers saw an intriguing tussle between Derek Bell and Clay Regazzoni, while BMW gave some added spice to the Formula by producing, at last, a cross flow four-valve engine which proved to be a winner straight from the box.

The Bell-Regazzoni duel lasted all season. Both drivers began determined to put the frustrations of the previous year behind them, and Bell's Wheatcroft Brabham took maximum points at Thruxton, finishing third overall behind the inevitable Rindt and Stewart. Regazzoni could only manage eighth after a spin. The next round was another dangerous slipstreaming affair at Hockenheim, the circuit again coming in for criticism (resulting in chicanes being placed on the straights later in the year). The first heat saw some frantic dicing for the lead between Bell, Regazzoni, Ikuzawa (Lotus) and Hahne (BMW): the Japanese driver won after blocking and weaving on the last lap, while Regazzoni forced his way past Bell at the Sachskurve to demote the Brabham driver to third. In the second heat, it was Hahne's turn to be the bad boy, the BMW weaving dangerously on the straights in an attempt to prevent others from passing, but Regazzoni passed Ikuzawa and Hahne on the last lap to claim the heat and be awarded overall victory over Ikuzawa by a scant 0.3 seconds on aggregate times. Bell was third.

The Middlesex driver scored an un-challenged win at the next championship round at the Barcelona Montjuich Park circuit, while Regazzoni's Tecno dropped from third to eighth after encountering metering problems four laps from home.

Derek Bell (Wheatcroft Racing Brabham-Cosworth BT30) challenged strongly throughout the season for championship honours. **23**

The duel between Clay Regazzoni (Tecno-Cosworth 70) and Dieter Quester (BMW 270) at the final Hockenheim round: the Austrian won the race on the last lap, but the Swiss became European Champion.

This gave Derek Bell an eleven-point lead in the championship, but after the next round, held at Rouen in June, the gap was reduced to four points. At the fast and dangerous French circuit, Jo Siffert, in the streamlined BMW, and Ronnie Peterson (March) enjoyed memorable dices both in their qualifying heat and in the final, when Peterson, in front, locked his rear brakes entering the Nouveau Monde hairpin on the penultimate lap and spun down to sixth. Siffert, therefore, scored his first F2 victory, with Clay Regazzoni finishing second to take maximum non-graded points. Similarly, BMW's first win after three years of trying had been claimed by Hubert Hahne at a non-championship race at Hockenheim a fortnight earlier.

The following month, Tecno introduced their new wide-nosed car for the inaugural international meeting at the safety-orientated Paul Ricard circuit near Marseilles. Clay Regazzoni enhanced his growing reputation (by now he had made his F1 début for Ferrari) with a convincing win after Siffert's and Ickx's BMW challenge faded. This battle was renewed in August at Enna, the circuit's new chicane not preventing slip-streaming as had been hoped. In a two-heat affair, Regazzoni pipped Siffert for the first heat by 0.3 seconds, with Ickx a further tenth of a second behind! The second heat was even closer, the two Swiss drivers being given identical race times at the end of it, which meant that Regazzoni was pronounced overall winner by virtue of his Tecno's superiority in the first heat. Derek Bell was classified seventh after coming in with his Brabham to fix a loose oil pipe, so now Regazzoni led his championship rival by 29 points to 27.

The début of BMW's torquier, parallel-valved engine was made at the non-championship Salzburgring meeting later that month, Ickx's overall victory underlining the fact that the Bavarian company was fast becoming the team to beat in F2.

The championship resumed at Langenlebarn, an emotional race weekend beginning with most of the teams attending Jochen Rindt's funeral. The Tecnos proved fastest in practice, and Regazzoni easily won the first heat from a scrapping Jack Brabham (guest-driving the Coombs BT30 once more) and Jacky Ickx, while Cevert in the other Tecno dropped from 2nd to 5th in the last eight laps with an engine misfire — just managing to hold off Bell's Brabham at the flag. In the second heat, Regazzoni retired with a rod through his engine after only five laps, leaving Ickx's BMW in the lead being chased by Brabham, with Cevert third in front of a battling Bell, Siffert and Peterson (March). Characteristically hunched over the steering wheel, Brabham closed on the German car at the rate of a half-second a lap, getting by at the chicane with nine laps to go. Then François Cevert decided on a big closing effort, passing Ickx and snatching the lead from Brabham three laps from the end. Brabham was still on target for an overall win, but on the last lap an injector pipe broke, and Ickx got by and pulled away sufficiently to take that from the Australian veteran as well. Siffert in the other BMW (Hubert Hahne failed to show for this event, thereby ending his association with the team and with motor racing) suffered a head-on collision with a straw-bale after being momentarily blinded by dust and a low sun, so Derek Bell finished fourth in the heat and was also classified fourth overall. With Cevert the only non-graded driver ahead, the six points gave Bell a four-point lead in the championship with two races to go.

The next round, on the demanding Imola circuit (hosting F2 cars for the first time) proved equally exciting. The Brambilla brothers made the best of their local knowledge and put their Brabhams amongst the leading contenders in the early stages, but the first heat developed into a battle between Regazzoni and the ever-improving Emerson Fittipaldi (Lotus), the Tecno driver regaining the lead on the last lap only to exit the Rivazza corner wide, with the clever Brazilian slipping through to win. The start of the second heat was delayed for five minutes whilst Clay's car was improved and sure enough this time the Tecno led from start to finish, although nearly caught by Ickx's hard-charging BMW at the end. The Swiss, therefore, claimed another overall win and maximum points, with Bell classified third behind Fittipaldi, the Wheatcroft Brabham having suffered clutch difficulties.

Championship rules this year stipulated that drivers could only count their best five performances, so Derek Bell could only add two points to his score, making him three points behind Regazzoni. October's Hockenheim meeting would decide it all.

As it turned out, Bell had a miserable weekend at the German track. To begin with, the Wheatcroft transporter was delayed, and Derek began practice in a spare BMW — until a rear tyre deflated on one of the straights and the car was pitched into the armco. Finally, in his familiar Brabham, Bell posted tenth fastest time — five places behind Regazzoni on the grid. Whilst in the race the Tecno sped away with the leading group, Bell missed out on the all-important tow and finished a lonely sixth. At the front, Regazzoni led from Quester's BMW going into the last lap, but the Austrian pulled alongside on the final straight and both cars touched entering the stadium, straying on to the infield, the BMW driver recovering quickest to take his first F2 win from the new European Champion.

1970 had seen a wealth of close racing and a bevy of new talent — Emerson Fittipaldi (who came third in the championship and was man-of-the-moment at Hockenheim following his Watkins Glen victory for Lotus in only his fourth Grand Prix) and managed a string of good results towards the end of the season when his ungainly March was more developed) being at the forefront. François Cevert had maintained his promise, claiming a win at the new Mantorp Park circuit in Sweden. More often than not he was the unluckiest of the works Tecno drivers, although he was fortunate to emerge unhurt from a 150mph excursion at Imola.

John Watson impressed again too, running third development times in the works March 712, and François Cevert, who would once again be at the wheel of the Tecno, the chassis steadily developed since 1968, this year featuring Tecno's own Pederzani-produced derivative of the four-valve Ford RS1600 engine in the back. Other possibles for the title were Dieter Quester, who had managed to persuade BMW to provide their engine solely for his Eifelland-entered March, and Tim Schenken and Carlos Reutemann, upholding the Brabham honours in their respective works and Automóvil Club Argentina-funded BT36 spaceframes. Emerson Fittipaldi would have been another strong contender but for his 1970 US Grand Prix win, which rendered him a graded driver and ineligible for European Championship points.

For the first time in the Formula, Brabham was not the main constructor, March's winter performances accounting for the production of 21 chassis by mid season. Apart from running at one point at Thruxton and setting fastest practice time at Montjuich, before crashing at Crystal Palace and Rouen, his Brabham puncturing on the flat-out Virage de Gresil and the Ulsterman breaking an arm and leg. Dieter Quester also showed he was a man to watch, following Hockenheim with a second win at Neubiberg. At this event, the BMW personnel wore black armbands, for the company's management had announced the firm's decision to quit motor racing, just as the success they had striven for for so long was being achieved.

1971 – A New King

The final year of the 1600cc F2 (the Formula was to be upped to 2 litres from 1972 in order to provide a clearer stepping-stone between F3 and the 3-litre F1) was marked by a vast number of would-be contestants — proving that F2 was as popular with drivers as it was with spectators. With generally oversubscribed entries (some events attracted as many as 50 applications), there was fierce competition simply to get on the starting grid, while Cosworth faced understandable servicing problems and a consequent shortage of spare engines. The championship was increased by three rounds to make 11 races in all at Hockenheim, Nürburgring (Germany); Thruxton, Crystal Palace (England); Jarama (Spain); Rouen and Albi (France); Mantorp Park (Sweden); Langenlebarn (Austria); and two events on consecutive weekends at Vallelunga (Italy); and there were a further eight non-championship meetings as well.

Championship favourites at the start of the season were Ronnie Peterson, who had achieved some astonishing (and well-publicised) winter

François Cevert proved a revelation at the wheel of the Pederzani BDA-powered Tecno 71, only to be let down by the car's unreliability.

Peterson, the works prepared cars for F3 graduates Mike Beuttler and Jean-Pierre Jarier, F2 veteran Jean-Pierre Jaussaud and the young Austrian Niki Lauda, all of whom effectively bought their drives in the form of sponsorship or petrol contracts. Against this purse-string operation, the Automóvil Club Argentina and a number of Argentine interests pooled a huge budget of £100,000 to back Reutemann and compatriot Carlos Ruesch — money which no doubt Frank Williams wished he had at his disposal for the March 712s he was entering for his Motul/Politoy team of Henri Pescarolo, Derek Bell and Brazilian Carlos Pace. Sticking with Brabham were Peter Westbury, John Watson and the Brambilla brothers, while Rondel Racing planned to run Graham Hill and Frenchman Bob Wollek as well as Schenken.

The brothers Fittipaldi found Bardahl sponsorship for their Lotus 69s, while Reine Wisell, François Migault, Gerry Birrell and Tetsu Ikuzawa campaigned similar machines. Jean-Pierre Jabouille and Patrick Depailler backed up Cevert in the Elf-sponsored Tecno team, whilst Helmut Marko, Jo Siffert and Jean-Pierre Beltoise headed the F2 efforts of Lola, Chevron and Pygmée.

The season looked like going Tecno's way at first. With a 15bhp advantage over the Cosworth FVAs, the Italian cars were well up in practice for the opening championship round at Hockenheim, and François Cevert won the first heat and came third in the second slipstreamer to take overall victory and nine championship points. At Thruxton, Cevert could only manage fourth place thanks to an engine misfire, but at the third round at the Nürburgring he achieved another win once race leader Derek Bell's oil pressure dropped and Ronnie Peterson (who'd already lowered the lap record twice) went off, blinded by dust and grit thrown up by Cevert's Tecno as he avoided the stricken Englishman.

This gave Cevert 22 points and a commanding ten-point championship lead, but thereafter his Tecno suffered enormous reliability problems and his tally was not added to for the remainder of the year.

Peterson, meanwhile, had begun the season spectacularly with a 120mph write-off when easily leading the non-championship Mallory Park meeting, and at Hockenheim retired with broken piston rings after setting fastest lap.

The Easter Monday meeting at Thruxton proved a memorable affair once again, featuring a titanic struggle for victory between the aspiring Peterson and old maestro Graham Hill in the Rondel Brabham. Hill had established a comfortable lead in the final when an exhaust pipe came adrift and his FVA lost power, so that — with just under 20 laps remaining — the yellow SMOG

Graham Hill (Rondel Racing Brabham-Cosworth BT36) leads Ronnie Peterson (March-Cosworth 712) into the chicane during their memorable dice at Thruxton.

March had narrowed the gap and was right on his tail. The former World Champion calmly held the attentions of Peterson at bay until, two laps from home, the Swede made his big effort entering the chicane and took the lead. But it was not over yet: on the last lap Ronnie got into a mix-up when overtaking a backmarker, going onto the grass, and the wily Hill slipped past again to clinch the Jochen Rindt Memorial Trophy by 0.6 seconds. Peterson, who'd earlier described Thruxton as dull because the back section of the circuit could now be taken flat out, had no complaints about the race!

With the works March driver suffering retirements in the next couple of championship rounds, the challenge to Cevert's lead was taken up by Carlos Reutemann, the Argentinian finishing third at the Nürburgring (second non-graded driver) and repeating this result at Jarama the same month after Tim Schenken, who had dominated the race in his Rondel Brabham, retired without oil pressure just three laps from the flag, handing victory to Fittipaldi's Lotus. The race was also notable for the performance of the unique Eiffeland March-BMW, which Quester forcefully drove into second place. A fifth place at Crystal Palace (fourth non-graded driver as victory once again went to Emerson Fittipaldi) brought Reutemann to within a point of the luckless Cevert.

The Tecno leader and Dieter Quester advanced their claims by winning the next two non-championship races, Quester's win at the Monza Gran Premio Lotteria being particularly exciting as

it was achieved by just 0.82 seconds after two closely-fought heats on the slipstreaming circuit.

All aspirants were silenced, however, and F2 enthusiasts proclaimed a new King when Ronnie Peterson secured four overall victories in the next five championship events. At Rouen and Mantorp Park, the Swede was involved in direct battles with Cevert, still his main rival if only his Tecno would hold together. On both occasions, François got in front of the March, only to crash with a locked crownwheel and pinion on the French circuit and retire with a dropped valve in Sweden after convincingly winning the first race in the two-heat contest. Peterson went on to win both rounds, setting fastest lap in the process on his home circuit.

Having dominated two more non-championship races at Kinnekulle and Brands Hatch (where F3 driver James Hunt made his F2 début in one of the rent-a-drive Marches), Peterson arrived for the next championship race on the Langenlebarn airfield circuit full of confidence. Despite heavy rain and drivers' worries about the straw-bale 'safety' measures on the track, the yellow March 712 led Heat 1 from start to finish. In Heat 2, however, it was Tim Schenken who made the running, until the closing laps saw Peterson driving hard to close the gap and then pressuring the Australian into a spin on the final lap, the Swede's last-minute win giving him a commanding championship lead.

The championship result was put beyond doubt at the penultimate round at Vallelunga. In the hot Italian sunshine, the circuit proved highly abrasive, blistering and chunking the F2 tyres in practice, and Reutemann — lying second in the points table — chose to run patterned tyres in the two-heat event whilst the others remained on slicks. It was the wrong decision, the Argentinian only managing fifth place in the first heat, while the other two championship contenders, Cevert and Schenken, both dropped out in an accident caused by the Tecno's water header tank splitting, and Peterson (minus fourth gear) took a secure second place behind Fittipaldi's Lotus. Reutemann improved to third in the second heat, but this time Fittipaldi's throttle cable snapped and Peterson drove to a heat win and overall victory. Ronnie's press-on, sideways style of driving his March had been strongly reminiscent of the great Jochen Rindt, and the new European Champion had endeared himself to F2 fans everywhere.

Apart from the performance of Peterson, Cevert and Reutemann (overall victor of the October non-championship race at Hockenheim), F2 could boast of several other promising showings. Peterson's old rival, Reine Wisell, scored a lucky win at Pau after Beltoise (guest-driving in Lauda's March) retired with just three laps remaining, but thereafter put most of his energies into legal disputes between himself and the LIRA-Team Lotus set-up. Carlos Pace, drafted into the Frank Williams March team from mid-season, managed an excellent third place in his début at the June non-championship Vallelunga meeting and followed this up with a win at Imola the following month — only his fourth F2 race!

Mike Beuttler impressed at the two Vallelunga races at the end of the season, finishing fourth overall in the first event and then winning the second (whose entry suffered from the championship having been decided the previous weekend) by fending off a determined Dieter Quester. American CanAm and F5000 luminary John Cannon put in some impressive drives early in the year, while John Watson continued to show promise in his old BT30 and young Niki Lauda did enough to secure the No. 1 March drive for 1972.

Among those keen to forget the 1971 season were Chevron and Lola, both of whose cars suffered from lack of development, and 1970 Championship contender Derek Bell who managed just one third placing for the Williams team, but fortunately was beginning to make an impact with the John Wyer team in sportscar racing.

1972 — Victory on Four Wheels

For 1972, all the signs were that F2 would continue to go from strength to strength. March was again the most popular marque, with a two-car works set-up for Niki Lauda and Ronnie Peterson and numerous machines for private entrants, including John Coombs/Elf (running François Cevert and Jean-Pierre Jabouille), and Shell Arnold (Jean-Pierre Beltoise and Jarier). Brabham — taken over by Bernie Ecclestone during the winter — planned their first production monocoque, the BT38, for a four-car Motul Rondel Racing team (featuring two graded drivers — Tim Schenken and Henri Pescarolo — plus Carlos

One of the fancied runners to suffer from engine problems during the first season of the 2-litre Formula was Niki Lauda (March-RES BDA 722), although the Austrian was pronounced John Player British F2 Champion.

Reutemann and Bob Wollek), with the French ASCA team (with veteran Jean-Pierre Jaussaud and Polish Count Adam Potocki) and Ed Reeves Racing (running Formula Atlantic/F3 graduate Dave Morgan) heading their privateer customers. Emerson Fittipaldi was keen to retain a Lotus involvement in the Formula, although it seemed he would have to content himself with the old Lotus 69 for one more season. Chevron intended making a real effort this year, again with Peter Gethin at the wheel, while Pygmée were involved in an ambitious four-car team, BERT, run by Rod Banting and Mike Earle and entering Derek Bell, Carlos Pace and fellow Brazilian Lian Duarte as well as the perennial Patrick Dal Bo.

Tecno found themselves too preoccupied with their F1 efforts to maintain a presence in F2, while Lola decided to give the new season a miss, but several new constructors were eager to take their place. Possibly the most potent newcomer was Team Surtees, who had obtained sponsorship from Matchbox Toys to run one of their typical square-sided monocoques, the TS10, for un-graded F1 driver Mike Hailwood and Big John himself. After four years away from the Formula, McLaren were to return with the Ralph Bellamy-designed M21 for Jody Scheckter, while F3 constructors GRD and Ensign planned occasional F2 sorties. Two interesting one-offs would be the Alan McCall-designed Tui and the French Alpine-built Elf 2 added to John Coombs' March strength. At the same time, the championship was increased to 15 rounds, with four non-championship races, and John Player were sufficiently keen to re-establish a British F2 Championship.

However, the Formula's glittering promise became somewhat tarnished as the season wore on and it was quickly realised that the CSI's decision to go for a 2-litre base was premature and ill-conceived.

The only engine which fulfilled the CSI's regulations, allowing for saloon car homologated engines of up to 2000cc, of which 1000 had had to have been made, was the four-valve Ford BDA engine produced for the Escort RS1600 and used in its 1½-litre form by Tecno the previous year.

But the BDA's block was never intended to be extended to 2-litre capacity. Ford produced special Siamese blocks (with larger jackets round the bores and no water channels between the first and second and the third and fourth cylinders), which enabled the engine to be bored out to approaching 1900cc, and planned to introduce an aluminium block version of the BDA which could run happily at the full 2 litres. However, the latter was homologated too late for use in the 1972 European season, and so the F2 runners were reliant on the varying efforts of several engine preparation concerns to extract as much power as possible from the BDA whilst trying to maintain reliability.

For several, this situation ended in disaster, engine blow-ups being an expensive business. Shell Arnold lost both their British mechanics and Jean-Pierre Jarier as the team's cash ran out; Peter Bloore's March entries for Mike Beuttler and Hiroshi Kazato did not complete the championship; the BERT Pygmée set-up disintegrated by mid-season; and several privateers were reduced to infrequent appearances through engine problems. A continual shortage of raceworthy engines afflicted the Formula throughout the season. Niki Lauda's and March's championship hopes vanished through reliance on the 1930cc motors of over-committed Race Engine Services (RES), while the much-publicised Amon Engines, linking the talents of engine development engineer Aubrey Woods and F1 driver Chris Amon, was wound up before the season ended after excruciating results both on the test bed and the race track.

The exceptions to the rule were Brian Hart's BDAs and the very limited production Cosworth BDF. Hart — with a lot of experience of BDAs in Escorts — agreed just before the start of the season to supply 1850cc engines, which gained in reliability what they lost in top-end power, although the Siamese blocks tended to crack and by the end of the season Hart was reduced to providing 1800cc blocks only. Cosworth made just four 1930cc BDFs, selling one each to March, Brabham (used by Rondel), Lotus and McLaren; although very quick when working, they were eventually ruined by a block problem, and there was a long delay before an improved version followed.

The season began unpredictably with a win at Mallory Park for young Dave Morgan, driving Ed Reeve's 1971 F3 Brabham BT35 chassis fitted with an 1800cc BDA and some old, narrow Firestones. Only 24 of the expected 43 entries showed up, partly because of the engine shortage and partly because Ecclestone's Brabham take-over had delayed development of the BT38, only Rondel's Reutemann and Wollek receiving their mounts in time. At the next round at Thruxton, championship favourite Reutemann suffered a nasty crash in practice when a stub axle sheared rounding Allards flat-out: the Argentinian broke an ankle which would put him out of action for two months, and suddenly the championship seemed wide open.

By round six, the situation was no clearer. Following Morgan's win at Mallory, the next four races had produced different maximum points scorers — Lauda at Thruxton (behind Peterson and Cevert), Jaussaud at Hockenheim, Gethin at Pau and Scheckter at Crystal Palace. The latter event (the last international meeting to be held on the tiny London circuit) featured a nail-biting duel between Scheckter's McLaren and the Surtees of Mike Hailwood during the final, by which time the track had become very slippery indeed. The McLaren led initially, Scheckter outbraking Hailwood into the first corner, but the Surtees fought its way to the front by lap 12, Scheckter falling further behind after a moment at North Tower eight laps later. The young South African determinedly hauled himself back to within two seconds of Hailwood, whose anti-roll bar broke nine laps from the end, creating braking problems. The former motorcycle champion did all he could to keep Scheckter behind him, but the McLaren squeezed past three laps from the flag to win by just over two seconds.

The next three races — at Hockenheim, Rouen and the Österreichring (Tulln Langenlebarn having lost its traditional F2 date) — saw consecutive wins for Emerson Fittipaldi in his BDF-powered Lotus 69, sponsored by Colin Chapman's Moonraker Yachts concern, while the championship developed into a battle between runners-up Jaussaud (second at Hockenheim) and Hailwood and Reutemann (second and third respectively in both France and Austria). Hailwood consolidated his reputation as a tryer at Rouen, where he diced for the lead with Fittipaldi for the first 20 laps of the 30-lap final. Following a spin at the hairpin, which dropped him 7.5 seconds behind the Lotus, Hailwood's yellow-and-blue Surtees came back at the rate of a second per lap, setting a new circuit record, until on lap 25, the car spun again.

Fifteen engines had been destroyed during practice and racing for the Hockenheim event, and the high mortality rate persisted at later rounds, the engine builders blaming the use of low-grade fuel for similar occurrences at the Österreichring. After the Austrian race, a crack was discovered in Fittipaldi's BDF engine block, and, with the last of the BDFs gone from the scene, the Hart-engined Surtees enjoyed consistently good results, finishing first and fourth (Surtees and de Adamich) at Imola; first and fifth (Hailwood and Ruesch) at Mantorp Park — where Gethin in the Chevron put on another fine showing before his retirement; third (Ruesch) at Enna, Hailwood winning the first heat and retiring when leading the second; and first and second (Hailwood and Pace) at the Salzburgring.

Brazilian Carlos Pace — driving for Surtees from August as a result of the BERT Pygmée debacle — made a significant impression, starting from the front of the grid at both Enna and the Salzburgring, where he contributed to an excellent Surtees 1–2, but it was the gritty Mike Hailwood who headed the championship with three rounds remaining. A win at Albi would have given Hailwood the title, but in his eagerness he went off the course whilst leading, handing the race to Jean-Pierre Jaussaud (ASCA Brabham), now his sole championship rival. The next race at Hockenheim (the last in the series, in fact, as Vallelunga was cancelled) went to the graded Tim Schenken, running a revised BDF in his Rondel Brabham, but Jaussaud retired with a broken driveshaft whilst Hailwood finished second to score maximum points and claim his first four-wheeled championship laurels.

The dire engine situation had badly affected

Jody Scheckter scored McLaren's only F2 European Championship victory at Crystal Palace, his Cosworth BDF-engined M21 gaining the lead just three laps from home.

Leading graded and non-graded drivers Emerson Fittipaldi (Lotus-Cosworth BDF 69) ahead of European Champion Mike Hailwood (Surtees-Hart BDA TS10) at Rouen.

what had seemed a promising year for the Formula, and had dashed many drivers' hopes for success. Nevertheless, among the newcomers who made their mark were Jochen Mass, who, driving a works March, defeated Derek Bell at an excellent non-championship Eifelrennen on the Nürburgring; Gerry Birrell, who managed a number of strong showings in Rodney Bloor's March-Hart; Jean-Pierre Jabouille (particularly when driving the Coombs March instead of the troublesome Elf); and James Hunt, who put a year-old March on the front row at Salzburg and then fought an epic duel with maestro Ronnie Peterson at the final British Championship round at Oulton Park, getting ahead of the Swede four laps from home, only to spin down to third. Niki Lauda had to content himself with the one-and-only John Player British F2 title, the cigarette sponsors deciding not to continue supporting the Formula after such a patchy year. John Watson impressed with guest drives for Tui (whose initial driver, New Zealander Bert Hawthorne, was killed at the April Hockenheim meeting) and Chevron, while veteran Graham Hill scored his last international victory at the non-championship Monza Lotteria in June.

1973 – Unbeatable BMW

To rid the Formula of the engine problems which had dogged it throughout 1972, the FIA agreed new regulations permitting 100-off cylinder heads for the following season, opening the door to engines from BMW, Lotus and Opel as well as the Ford BDA, and its Pinto variant developed by Holbay.

The strongest challenge to the alloy block BDA was likely to be the 275bhp 16-valve BMW engine which had already been used successfully in saloon and sportscar racing. Max Mosley pulled off a coup by agreeing a deal with the German firm, whereby works BMW engines would only be supplied with March chassis in 1973, thereby initiating a partnership which was to dominate F2 for a far longer period. Heading the works March effort would be the ebullient Jean-Pierre Jarier – up from their F3 team –supported by former European Champion Jean-Pierre Beltoise (incredibly non-graded again following a disastrous 1972 season) when available and by BMW's up and coming Hans Stuck. The compact March-BMW 732 was also sold to privateers Brian Lewis (for Colin Vandervell and Mike Beuttler), Filipinetti (Jacques Coulon), the Brambilla brothers and Formula Atlantic champion Bill Gubelmann.

Team Surtees decided to keep faithful to the BDA engines of Brian Hart, who used his F2 experience to restrict the number of motors to be maintained by him during the year. Jochen Mass was the team's hope to follow in Mike Hailwood's wheeltracks, with a second works car usually reserved for graded drivers – Hailwood himself or Carlos Pace. Other Hart customers were Chevron (running Peter Gethin and Gerry Birrell in the straightforward B25 model) and Coombs Elf (a development of last year's spaceframe for Patrick Depailler and Jean-Pierre Jabouille).

Rondel Racing were to field a huge five-car team for Jody Scheckter, Bob Wollek, Jean-Pierre Jaussaud and graded drivers Tim Schenken and Henri Pescarolo. This year, the set-up would run

Jean-Pierre Jarier had an astonishingly successful 1973 season, taking his March-BMW 732 to seven race wins.

the Ray Jessop-designed Motul M1 (designated after the team's main sponsors) powered by Ford FVD engines — a development of the FVC sportscar motor.

Other dependants of the FVD were the flamboyant Pierre Robert team from Sweden, running GRDs for Reine Wisell and Sten Gunnarson. GRD themselves planned to support a substantial number of their F2 cars entered by privateer teams, notably Wheatcroft Racing (for Roger Williamson) and Team Nippon (Hiroshi Kazato and Tetsu Ikuzawa), powered by BDAs from various tuning establishments.

The works Brabham BT40 was entrusted to John Watson, and Patrick Dal Bo and François Migault were to pilot the latest Pygmée MDB18s, while the Formula welcomed three newcomers: the Patrick Head-designed Scott, commissioned by driver Richard Scott; the Royale for Lichtenstein's Manfred Schurti; and last but not least the Lotus 74, christened the Texaco Star — Lotus' first F2 chassis for four years, powered by the Novamotor-developed Lotus engine and driven by the F1 Lotus pairing of Emerson Fittipaldi and Ronnie Peterson.

With such a healthy interest in the Formula, the FIA decided to organise the championship to involve all 22 F2 events planned for the season: 12 of these meetings would count as basic events, whilst the remaining ten would be optional, with drivers able to compete in four such races (providing they were in different countries) in the hope of adding to their basic points score. This complex arrangement proved to be financially disastrous, particularly in relation to a stagnant prize money scale which meant that most entrants stood to lose £1000 per car per race unless they were attracting maximum trade bonuses, finishing in the first two or three or running graded 'name' drivers. In the end, five of the planned meetings were cancelled, a number of events were poorly supported both by entrants and (in response) the public, and privateers in particular found it impossible to continue in the Formula.

From the very first meeting — a non-basic race at Mallory Park in March — it was obvious that March-BMW had got their sums right. The BMW engine enjoyed more torque than its Ford-based rivals, and the Marches were by far the quickest out of corners, Beltoise and Jarier setting the fastest practice times. On raceday, Jarier dominated both heats in the two-part event, taking a two-second lead at the end of lap 1 of the second heat and continuing to drive on the limit to the chequered flag.

Two other of the new BMW engines were involved in spectacular blow-ups, Beltoise's showering the pit lane as his car crossed the start/finish line, and Vandervell's exploding with such force on the back of the circuit that Jarier's March, following, lost its airbox to flying shrapnel.

At almost £5000 a time, the loss of an engine could pose a serious financial problem to a March entrant, but the Mallory incidents were traced to incorrect pistons, and, except for an initial tendency to overheat and a batch of defective relief valves later in the season, BMW managed to maintain a fair degree of reliability for the rest of the year. Jarier, indeed, suffered no engine problems whatsoever and took the European Championship by storm, recording seven wins, two seconds and a tenth placing (after throttle linkage problems) and two crashes from 12 starts. A naturally exuberant personality, Jarier's dominance of the Formula was unquestionable: in the style of Jim Clark, the Frenchman appeared to want to win races from the front and by as clear a margin as possible, although for Jarier this entailed driving the March on the limit throughout. The two accidents occurred in consecutive rounds early in the season, Jarier's March being involved in a startline melée at Thruxton and then spinning off after hitting puddles whilst leading at the Nürburgring: at the next round at Pau, Max Mosley threatened Jarier (starting the final from the back of the grid) with the sack if he attempted to snatch the lead during the first lap(!), and Jean-Pierre drove steadily to finish second to Cevert's Elf and claim maximum championship points.

The only occasion on which Jarier had a real fight for the lead on his hands occurred at a non-basic event on the Swedish circuit of Karlskoga in August, when Firestone produced some new compounds which threatened Goodyear's superiority. The March driver made yet another perfect start to lead the 48-lap final, but a broken nose spoiler affected the March's downthrust and caused braking problems so that, by lap 30, local man Torsten Palm (in a hired works Surtees) and Peter Gethin (Chevron) had closed right up. Two laps later, Gethin was second after Palm missed a gearchange, and the rest of the race saw a titanic struggle between the troubled March and the Chevron, with Palm in the Surtees also looking for a way by. Using the torque of his BMW engine to pull away on the straight, Jarier dived into corners on the inside lane, frequently locking up under braking, to keep Gethin at bay by a scant 0.2 seconds, Palm finishing third and setting fastest lap.

The only driver who seemed likely to compete on equal terms with Jarier was English F3 Champion Roger Williamson, his team, Wheatcroft Racing, jettisoning their troublesome GRD for a March-BMW in mid-season in order to try for outright victories. The Wheatcroft March's début was at Rouen in June, when the death of works Chevron driver Gerry Birrell in practice, after a head-on crash into some loosely-fitted armco, led to drivers demanding overnight alterations to the circuit: Williamson led his heat conclusively despite a misfire until loss of oil pressure intervened and the car had to be retired for the day. Three days later at Monza, however, after an overnight drive and just 12 flying laps on a circuit he'd never raced on before, Williamson claimed pole position for the F2 Lotteria, run in two 20-lap heats. Getting away third in the first heat, Roger disposed of Mass (Surtees) on lap 5 and then outbraked leader Vittorio Brambilla (March-BMW) into a chicane on lap 11 to go away and win by 11.03 seconds, with Patrick Depailler's Elf finishing runner-up. At the start of the second heat, Depailler, Brambilla and Williamson entered the first chicane abreast, the two Marches touching, taking to the escape road and restarting at the rear of the small eleven-car field. By the end of the lap, Williamson and Brambilla had recovered to seventh and eighth places, but Depailler was leading over 30 seconds ahead – a more than adequate margin for overall victory. While Brambilla spun again, the Englishman pressed on, claiming fourth on lap 3, third on lap 4 and second on lap 6. With Depailler making a mistake at one of the chicanes and his Elf developing a misfire, Williamson gradually reeled him in, only to resort to an escape road once more after outbraking the leader: this time, Roger kept his foot down, a startled marshal rapidly raised the exit barrier, and the March rejoined the track just three lengths behind the French car! On the following lap, Williamson made no mistake in

overtaking Depailler to win both the second heat and the Lotteria itself.

The next F2 event was a non-championship affair at Misano, and here Williamson and the March impressed again, the combination heading the first heat until electrical failure intervened, and then catching and passing the Fittipaldi brothers to win the second heat and take sixth place overall. However, the long-awaited confrontation between Jarier (who'd been absent at these races) and Williamson in March-BMWs never occurred, for later that month the talented Englishman was killed in a fiery accident during the Dutch Grand Prix – his second F1 race in a Wheatcroft-hired works March-Ford.

Behind Jarier, F2 remained a close-run, cut-and-thrust affair, with a number of other notable performances during the year. Jochen Mass took the Surtees to win at Kinnekulle (in front of eight other cars – the smallest ever field for a European Championship race) and the June Hockenheim meeting, and was usually quicker than the other March-BMW runners. Reine Wisell, now graded, chalked up GRD's only F2 win at a rain-soaked Nürburgring. Jacques Coulon, aided by a special Firestone compound, won the penultimate race of the season at Vallelunga, and then finished second to Jarier at Estoril the following weekend, while Vittorio Brambilla achieved everyone's ambition and actually beat Jarier at Albi, an earlier win at the Salzburgring being another highpoint in a remarkably consistent season for the Italian, once his brother, Tino, had announced his retirement. Bertil Roos showed well in a GRD hired by mentor Fred Opert for the Swedish

Roger Williamson looked to be the only driver likely to challenge Jarier once Wheatcroft Racing had acquired a March too, but the Englishman's career was cut tragically short by a fatal accident at the F1 Dutch Grand Prix.

A promising newcomer to F2, Tom Pryce put up a number of good drives in a Rondel Racing Motul M1.

rounds, enjoying a fine dice with Hailwood in his heat at Karlskoga.

Rondel Racing had a mixed year, Jody Scheckter leaving the team early on, but Henri Pescarolo scoring a fortunate win at Thruxton after Beuttler (March-BMW) and Birrell (Chevron) collided at the chicane just two laps from home, and Tim Schenken taking overall victory at the Norisring after an excellent dice with team-mate Tom Pryce, who, after joining the team in mid-season, often proved the fastest Motul runner. Following John Watson's bad crash in the F1 Race of Champions, Wilson Fittipaldi took over the wheel of the sole works Brabham, its only success coming at the poorly supported Misano meeting.

The Chevron effort was badly hit by the Birrell tragedy at Rouen, but thereafter Peter Gethin and a recovered John Watson kept the tiny Bolton firm in the picture.

The Elf team had a poor year, Depailler suffering a number of niggling problems and failing to chalk up a much-sought-for win. For Lotus, the season was even worse. The Nova motor-developed Lotus engine lacked both power and reliability, and the team was probably only continued as it benefited from the F2 financing arrangements by having both Peterson and Emerson Fittipaldi on its books. The Lotus-Texaco connection was apparently finally severed at Albi in September when Dave Morgan, in the second Texaco Star, failed to qualify after a variety of practice problems, while Peterson started the race from the pit road after water pump problems on the warming-up laps, only for the engine to give way within a few tours.

1974 – Three March Hares

After the March works' domination of the 1973 Championship, and with BMW engines becoming generally available for 1974, it was not difficult to guess the trend for the new season. To do well in 1974, it seemed you had to have a March-BMW, or at least a BMW motor.

Among the customers flocking to buy Marches (updates of Jarier's model) were Brian Lewis Racing, who were to run two cars for American Bill Gubelmann and the promising Andy Sutcliffe; the Trivelatto Racing Team, entering Gabriel Serblin and Giancarlo Martini, and their compatriots CSAI, bringing Maurizio Flammini and Duilio Truffo up from lesser formulas; Team Harper, wealthy Hong Kong businessman Bob Harper putting up the money for two cars for Dieter Quester (back from retirement) and David Purley; and BP France, backing French F3 Champion Jacques Lafitte together with Jean-Pierre Paoli. The works 742s would be entrusted to BMW favourite Hans Stuck, supported by Elf protégé Patrick Depailler (both of whom also secured regular F1 drives – Stuck for March and Depailler for Tyrell –before the F2 season commenced), whilst a third works-prepared car would run in Antar colours for Jacques Coulon.

Although the Ford BDG engine – developed by Hart and Cosworth – appeared the equal of the BMW powerplant, most of the March opposition elected to play safe and fit the German motors.

The main challenge to March looked like coming from the Elf-backed French Alpine set-up, which this year elected to run four Alpine A367s (referred to as Elf 2s) for Jean-Pierre Jabouille, Patrick Tambay, Michel Leclere and Alain

Serpaggi. The familiar tubular spaceframe chassis — the only competitive spaceframe left in contemporary motor racing — was modified to accept Josef Schnitzer's BMW engines (the team being unable to approach the works for motors due to a longstanding Alpine/BMW dispute), and again featured very effective aerodynamic bodywork. Chevron, too, would use Schnitzer-prepared engines, entrusting the Baty/Ottershaw Motors team to represent them with cars for James Hunt and Hiroshi Kazato, while the main Ford defectors were Team Surtees, who planned to fit factory BMWs to their T15A chassis for contracted driver John Watson and a Marlboro-Ecuador team run by former Rondel team manager Ron Dennis, which ended up hosting the only regular graded competitor in the series, Tim Schenken.

Smaller F2 efforts were those of GRD, building a new Hart-powered car for Belgian Claude Bourgoignie, and Kaimann of Germany, who were running an Opel-engined machine for Austrian Helmut Koinigg.

Having learnt their lesson from the plethora of races last year, the CSI this time envisaged a 14-round championship, of which 10 events — in Spain, Germany, France, Austria, Italy and Sweden — actually occurred. After the disappointing crowd figures of last year, and with the BARC failing to find a sponsor for their traditional Thruxton fixture, British race promoters felt unable to give the Formula their support.

Following his promising appearances in 1973, Hans Stuck was favourite to continue where Jarier had left off, and when the cars turned out for practice at the opening race at Montjuich,

Barcelona, the name of the game became even clearer: the works Marches bore little resemblance to the customer models, as they featured different suspension geometry and side radiators and F1-type nose-cones and brakes. Stuck and Depailler dominated practice and race, Jabouille's Elf finishing third with understeer problems while third man on the grid, Bertil Roos (in the Fred Opert Hart-powered Chevron B27, destined for a Formula Atlantic season in Canada) could not repeat his practice performance in the race, coming home eighth.

The next round at Hockenheim featured a larger entry than the Spanish race, four Elfs, four Surtees, two GRDs, two Chevrons, an old Brabham and the unique Kaimann (whose Opel engine blew at the start of practice, driver Helmut Koinigg transferring to a Surtees for the rest of the meeting) arriving to do battle with 21 Marches. Stuck and Depailler again annexed the front row of the starting grid, their nearest rivals Beltoise (substituting for Jabouille in an Elf) and Watson (driving last season's Surtees-Hart following recent fire damage to the Surtees transporter and cars). After dominating the first of the two 20-lap heats comprising the Jim Clark Memorial Race, the works March-BMWs didn't have it quite all their own way in the second, Depailler pitting with a loose nosecone, and Stuck slowing with a puncture, although still finishing some 17 seconds ahead of the battling Leclere (Elf-BMW) and Watson, who swopped positions behind the young German on the overall standings.

Patrick Depailler's smooth driving style proved more appropriate to the tricky street circuit

36   *March domination — the 742s of Hans Stuck and Patrick Depailler drive away from the field at Hockenheim.*

of Pau than his team-mate's erratic approach, the Frenchman — armed with superior Goodyear rain tyres — setting fastest practice time and winning convincingly the François Cevert Memorial Trophy (the former Tecno F2 driver had been killed at the previous year's American Grand Prix) once Stuck had crashed his car on lap 2. The race was notable for the strong showing of Jacques Laffite, who put his Tico Martini-bodied March-BMW onto the third grid slot and then enjoyed an extended duel with Leclere's Elf, diving past for second place at the hairpin on the last lap, Leclere spinning his car in the confusion and allowing a determined Andy Sutcliffe (Brian Lewis March-BMW) and Jean-Pierre Jabouille through for third and fourth. A sign of the times was that only non-starters prevented the race from becoming an all BMW-engined affair.

The singleton Ford runner at Pau, José Dolhem in the works Surtees TS15, managed even better at the fast Salzburgring track, charging up from the back of the field after a first lap melée, setting fastest lap and clinching second place from Quester and Purley (Team Harper now running new Chevron-BMWs in retaliation for the clear superiority of the works Marches over the customer models), only for Purley to nip ahead on the last lap when fuel pick-up problems intervened. This race also featured an impressive début of Team Baty's Schnitzer-engined Chevron, Josef Schnitzer removing his moustache to celebrate Tom Pryce's pole position with the car, and the Welshman leading before pitting on three cylinders. There then followed a furious scrap at the front between Jabouille's Elf and the Marches

of Stuck (up from a lowly 11th grid position) and Laffite, the BP France car taking its first win after the Elf stopped without oil and Stuck broke a gear linkage.

This result placed Laffite just three points behind the joint championship leaders, Stuck and Depailler (who failed to qualify in Austria following a huge crash in practice), and the French privateer managed to split the works drivers in the table after finishing second overall at the June Hockenheim meeting, which saw the first-ever race win for a Schnitzer BMW engine, nestling in the back of Jean-Pierre Jabouille's orange-topped Elf. The win was also Firestone's first of the year, the company having reverted to 23-inch diameter tyres as used by Roos at Barcelona to get back on equal terms with Goodyear.

With Stuck away racing a BMW touring car at the Nürburgring, Depailler regained the championship lead with an overall win at the new Mugello circuit in northern Italy. Laffite had won pole position, only to retire in the first heat with a blown engine, his teammate Jean-Pierre Paoli taking the second heat ahead of a confident Depailler, while Masami Kuwashima (March-BMW) retired with a broken wheel bearing after showing strongly in both events. Stuck's replacement, F3 March driver Brian Henton, managed sixth place on his F2 debut, while Tom Pryce improved on his Hockenheim fourth position by bringing the Baty Chevron-BMW home in third.

The rain-soaked non-championship Rouen meeting was dominated by Hans Stuck and smart pitwork by the March team, the German finishing almost a minute ahead of Purley's Chevron-BMW

Jacques Laffite (Martini March-BMW 742) and Michel Leclere (Elf-BMW 2) battle it out in the rain at Pau.

despite making three pit stops and changing nine tyres during the course of the race. James Hunt, finally at the wheel of the Baty Chevron, fell out of the race ignominiously after coming in and claiming that conditions were too dangerous to continue.

King Ronnie Peterson returned to the Formula for the Swedish Championship round on the narrow, twisty and bumpy Karlskoga track, passing Depailler just after one-third distance to head a works March 1–2, although fastest lap went to the Frenchman. With Stuck spinning from second to 16th early on, Jacques Laffite held off Tambay's Elf (which eventually crashed on its own oil) and Kuwashima to finish third and take enough points to again split Depailler and Stuck in the Championship table.

Thereafter, however, the BP France challenge faded, and it became evident that the championship honours would be decided between the two factory March pilots. The next round, at Enna, saw a number of nasty accidents caused by high kerbing at the circuit's unpopular chicanes: both Stuck and Depailler crashed in practice when their rear calipers locked, turning the cars sharply under braking into the kerbing, but both entries were repaired in time to take up their front row grid positions. Stuck easily won the first of the 30 lap heats once Watson had spun his Surtees-BMW, while Depailler suffered a fuel pump short and Laffite ran out of petrol. The latter's team made no such mistake in the second heat, Laffite winning, but Hans Stuck taking second despite two spins to regain second place in the championship just five points behind his teammate. Tom Pryce had a spectacular accident in this heat when the gearshift broke on his fourth-placed Chevron-BMW, the car somersaulting, landing astride the armco, splitting the monocoque, and finishing up in the lake on the inside of the track, the Welshman, miraculously, being unhurt.

The Elf-BMWs of Jabouille and Tambay (fresh from his non-championship win at Nogaro where René Arnoux was added to the team and finished a promising fourth) headed practice for the last Hockenheim fixture of the year, Jabouille taking the first 20-lap heat by 0.3 seconds from Depailler, with Laffite and Stuck fourth and fifth. In the second heat, Laffite's Championship hopes dived along with his oil pressure, while a sticking throttle caused Jabouille to spin away his lead in favour of Stuck, Depailler finishing second ahead of a storming young Swede, Gunnar Nilsson in Brian Lewis's March-BMW. The aggregate result gave victory to Depailler from Stuck, and so the two March drivers went into the last round at Vallelunga eight points apart, Stuck needing a win with his teammate failing to score in order to take the Championship.

As things turned out, the Italian event proved a benefit for Patrick Depailler's black March, the Frenchman again driving at his smooth best to claim pole position, win the first heat by 25 seconds and similarly dominate the second heat, while Stuck took a second and third to finish runner-up to his teammate in both the race and the championship. Jacques Laffite managed third overall, the race result summing up the story of the season.

1975 – Elf Sùrtout

Delighted by Depailler's championship win, the French petrol company Elf nevertheless found themselves with a problem when they considered where to give their support for the 1975 season. A steady nurturing of French talent in lesser formulas over the past eight years had left the government-owned company with too many promising drivers dependent on Elf sponsorship, and the world fuel crisis and economic recession which erupted in the winter of 1974 only made matters more complicated.

In the end, it was decided to spread the Elf finances between three teams. Michel Leclere and Patrick Tambay were brought together in the works March team to drive a new chassis, the 752 — a low, wide monocoque, very different from the Marches used in F2 over the past three years. Elf's prime candidate for championship honours was thought to be Jean-Pierre Jabouille, who was permitted to build his own car at the Alpine factory (Alpine now being too engrossed in their sports-car and turbo engine projects to mount a proper F2 effort themselves): called the Elf 2J, the car comprised a short-wheelbase, narrow-track tubular chassis clothed in aerodynamic bodywork and powered by a Schnitzer BMW engine. Alpine sportscar driver Gerard Larousse was chosen to support Jabouille, initially in last year's Alpine A367/Elf 2. Finally, the remaining Elf funds were distributed to Jacques Laffite and Tico Martini — the combination which had nearly won last year's championship, and this year would be running a singleton bulbous-looking Martini Mk16, also powered by the reverse inlet Schnitzer engine.

In the face of Elf's steamrollering policy and a general lack of finance to go motor racing, it was not surprising that support elsewhere for F2 lessened considerably. Surtees, GRD and Kaimann were gone for good, and only Chevron (a BDA-powered car for Hector Rebaque, a BMW-engined example for Harald Ertl, and two Chrysler-Simca cars for Jean-Pierre Beltoise, Christian Ethuin and Xavier Lapeyre) and the Italian Osella team (running Italian F3 Champion Giorgio Francia, Duilio Truffo and Arturo Merzario) accompanied the usual herd of privateer Marches on a

The story of the 1975 season: Elf-backed drivers Jean-Pierre Jabouille (Elf-BMW 2), Patrick Tambay (March-BMW 752) and Jacques Laffite (Martini-BMW Mk16) fight for the honours at Rouen.

regular basis. Formula Atlantic-based cars, the Wheatcroft R18, March 75B and Lola T360B, improved the field on occasions. Nevertheless, the number of European Championship rounds actually increased, there being 14 races this year. There was no Swedish or Spanish event on this occasion, but Rouen and Nogaro gained championship status and British interest revived with rounds at Thruxton and Silverstone once more.

By the end of the season, the Elf executives could proudly reflect on their F2 investment, their five drivers taking the first five places in the championship. The finishing order, however, was not as had been anticipated eight months earlier.

Although the experienced championship favourite, Jean-Pierre Jabouille, put his Elf on the front of the grid at six of the meetings, his season was punctuated by mechanical problems, particularly with the Schnitzer BMW engines. After a couple of low placings, he took his first win in his self-designed car at Magny-Cours (a non-championship event) after the works Marches had retired. His only championship win of the year came at the bland Salzburgring track, where the race was delayed for almost three hours after the drivers refused to go out until the circuit had dried from the effects of a hail storm just before the scheduled start. On this occasion, the Elf team leader drove to an untroubled win, although there weren't many spectators there to see it, as half the crowd had gone home by 6pm, when the race finally began! Thereafter, the engine problems increased, the result of Josef Schnitzer having taken on too much F2 servicing work: several privateers took their engines elsewhere by mid-season, and by the last race at Vallelunga, the Austrian company was in financial difficulties and threatening to withhold engines until bills had been paid. At the end of it all, Jabouille had to be content with fifth championship place.

His team-mate, Gerard Larousse, was more fortunate. At the wheel of last year's Alpine-built Elf 2 for most of the season, Larousse scored an aggregate win at the April Hockenheim meeting after highly competitive drives in both heats, and followed this with a fourth at Pau and a second at Enna — a race he almost won. Supplied with the second Elf 2J at the Silverstone round in August, the sportscar ace finished second after a drive at the head of the field. For most of the rest of the year, engine problems intervened, and so Larousse took fourth place in the championship.

The works March team had its difficulties too. The project was put off balance by the decision of Goodyear (now the sole tyre supplier in F2) at the start of the season to switch from 25in to 23in diameter rear tyres, while a lot of pre-season running with a Ford engine (some 45lb

lighter than the BMW motor) may have upset the 752's balance. Certainly, the car was too heavy and the rear suspension geometry unsatisfactory, leading to a tendency to suffer both from understeer and oversteer on tighter circuits. Neither Leclere nor Tambay were able to sort the cars, and on top of this, they suffered from engine unreliability at the beginning of the season, the factory Paul Rosche-developed BMWs initially suffering from soft tappet shims which caused valve spring breakages.

Prior to Rouen, in June, the team's best results were two second places by Tambay at Thruxton and the Nürburgring, but — with the cause of the engine failures discovered at the previous round — everything went right at the swooping French circuit, Leclere taking an easy first F2 win, with Tambay second just 6½ seconds behind after a brief tussle with Laffite. Incidents at Mugello and Enna kept the Marches out of the points, but at Silverstone, amidst a great struggle for the lead between Larrousse and Henton in the Wheatcroft, Leclere took advantage of a missed gear by Larrousse at Stowe, which baulked the British driver, to nip ahead for another victory. The Elf-sponsored round at Zolder saw another March 1-2, Leclere finishing ahead of Tambay, and the following race at Nogaro saw a reversal of the result, a calm and mature Patrick Tambay taking a finely-driven win from Leclere. With both drivers crashing at the last round at Vallelunga, they ended the season with exactly the same points; joint second.

And so the championship was taken by the tenacious Jacques Laffite driving Tico Martini's first F2 car. He gained a fortunate victory at the rainsoaked opening round at Estoril: Laffite recovered from a spin and a pit stop for slicks to wrest the race laurels from Swiss unknown Loris Kessel's March-BMW 742 when the latter's gear linkage broke up six laps from home. The French combination went on to score four more wins from the next five races. An overall win at Thruxton was followed by an exhilarating display at the Nürburgring, where the Martini claimed pole position with a time which would have seen it well up on the grid for the previous year's F1 Grand Prix. On this occasion, the Eifelrennen were divided into two 7-lap heats run on consecutive days: Laffite ran away with the first heat, despite losing his clutch at half-distance, and the next day — following no less than three clutch changes to the Martini — finished a comfortable second to the graded Hans Stuck (March-BMW) to claim another nine championship points.

The street circuit of Pau witnessed a classic struggle between Laffite and Jean-Pierre Jabouille, the two fastest men in practice. After causing the start to be delayed whilst some last-

Tico Martini's first F2 car brought Jacques Laffite the European Championship with six outright race wins.

minute ignition problems on the Martini were rectified, Laffite got away in the lead, only for his BMW engine to splutter going up the hill just enough for Jabouille's Elf to move ahead. For 62 of the race's 73 laps, Laffite continued to press the race leader, Jabouille finding it harder and harder to keep in front as the Elf's lightening fuel load led to increased brake bias: nine laps from the chequered flag, Jabouille got out of shape at the Station Hairpin, Laffite slipping past to win by 16 seconds.

Laffite decided to miss the Swedish Grand Prix for the June Hockenheim round in order to extend his F2 Championship lead with a further win, but thereafter the Martini team suffered from the Schnitzer malaise, the only relief being a narrow victory over Gerard Larousse at Enna after the works Marches had eliminated each other. Jacques clinched the championship at the next round at Silverstone, sitting in the pit lane with fuel injection problems while the Elf team failed to get the win they needed to maintain their championship hopes. A determined drive to second place at the season closer at Vallelunga despite throttle problems further enhanced

Laffite's reputation.

Against such overwhelming odds, it was not surprising that few other drivers managed to make much of an impact. Bespectacled Italian Maurizio Flammini was the only non-Elf driver to score a race win, coolly taking both heats of the July round on the demanding Mugello road circuit near Florence. Driving his previous year's March, the Italian managed further strong placings at Zolder and Vallelunga. Alessandro Pesenti-Rossi, Claude Bourgoignie and Hans Binder (March-BMWs), Harald Ertl (Chevron-BMW) and American Ted Wentz (converted Formula Atlantic Lola-BDG) impressed on occasions, but the only other consistent charger was Brian Henton, who kept the British flag flying whenever finances permitted. With the loan of the prototype March 752 and a Hart BDA motor, Brian led and set joint fastest lap at Thruxton before retiring and finished third at the April Hockenheim. For the Silverstone race, Tom Wheatcroft had his Mike Pilbeam-designed Formula Atlantic car converted to F2 specification, Henton getting onto the front row of the grid and coming home third after leading briefly and featuring strongly throughout. Such

41

Brian Henton (Wheatcroft-Hart BDA R18) got himself up amongst the Elfs with a storming drive at Silverstone: Jabouille leads, with Larrousse running third behind the Mike Pilbeam-designed car.

performances from Brian Henton were to continue to feature strongly in the Formula over the next few years.

1976 – Powered by Renault

Following three years' domination of F2 by the BMW production-based unit, 1976 saw the introduction of new rules permitting the use of pure racing engines, and teams turned to motors from Renault, Hart, Lancia Ferrari, Abarth, Chevrolet and Chrysler in attempts to end the Bavarian firm's run of success.

March, indeed, had fitted a Renault V6 engine – the most likely challenger – in a F2 chassis in the middle of the previous year as a development exercise, but had turned down the chance of using the French motor, preferring to stick with the BMW four-cylinder. Over the winter, BMW engineer Paul Rosche made a number of alterations to the engine, notably shorter injection trumpets, modified inlet ports and larger and longer pipes on the exhaust system, producing an extra 200 rpm. BMW hoped this would be sufficient to see off the Renault threat, and were adamant that they would not be drawn into the expensive business of constructing a racing engine should the four-cylinder prove uncompetitive. Maurizio Flammini and ex-March F3 driver Alex Ribeiro would steer the works March-BMWs, whilst a private 762 would be handled by Giancarlo Martini, whose Everest team had originally planned to put him in a F1 Ferrari for the season.

Other March privateers decided to run the all-alloy Hart 420R engine instead of the BMW. In existence since 1974, when it powered a Chevron sportscar, this four-cylinder motor was lighter than both the BMW and Renault and was particularly strong at its top end. Among the Harlow engine builder's customers were Willi Kauhsen's team, running Ingo Hoffmann and German saloon car ace Klaus Ludwig, while Fred Opert opted for both BMW and Hart-powered Chevron B35s, and another Hart was fitted to the back of Ian Grob's Modus entry.

Chevron Cars in fact could manage no works effort this year, but the straightforward B35 won its fair share of orders. Opert was the major customer, planning to enter a series of drivers, while Trivellato would run Roberto Marazzi in a Chevron-BMW and Harald Ertl also joined the Chevron ranks. Jean-Pierre Jaussaud would persevere with the ROC team's Chevron-Chrysler efforts.

Smaller, BMW-powered efforts were launched by Toj (running German-domiciled Finn Keke Rosberg), Lola (Germans Rolf Binder, Bertram Schäfer and Reinhold Jöst heading the T450 runners), Osella (Hans Binder and Giorgio Francia) and Ralt (for veteran Swede racer Freddy Kottulinsky), with the Van Hool and Amweg machines making one-off appearances in the hands of Bernard de Dryvver and Swiss Alfred Amweg respectively.

Turning their hopes to Italian powerplants were the Project Four team and Wheatcroft

René Arnoux proved a strong contender for championship honours in the Renault-engined Martini Mk19.

Racing. The former chose the Lancia Stratos Ferrari Dino V6 (developed by Tino Brambilla) to sit in the back of March 762s for Eddie Cheever and the graded Jochen Mass, while Brian Henton's Wheatcroft would this year run the Holbay-prepared straight six-cylinder Abarth motor.

The 305bhp Gordini Renault engine would power the Elf-sponsored teams of Martini (running Patrick Tambay and Super Renault champion René Arnoux) and Elf (Jean-Pierre Jabouille acquiring Michel Leclere as his team mate). Designed four years earlier, the 24-valve V6 had already helped Alpine-Renault to the 1974 European Sportscar Championship, and the two teams would be supplied with no less than two dozen of these engines.

With Silverstone and Zolder dropping out of the calendar, the European Championship became a 13-round affair with the addition of a third race at the Hockenheim circuit.

The pattern for the season was set right from the opening Hockenheim event, when both the Project Four March-Lancias failed to qualify through engine problems (Ferrari, supplier of the block and crankshafts, having apparently told Lancia to stick to rallying!) and the race was dominated by the March and Elf-backed teams. There was consternation when the cars arrived at the German circuit and police threatened to impound both Elf équipes as the Schnitzer brothers claimed they were owed money for spare parts supplied to the teams the previous season: both teams managed to produce the cash to enable them to race. Graded guests Hans Stuck and Ronnie Peterson annexed the front row of the grid for March-BMW, but it was Jabouille's Elf-Renault which made the early running before his V6 expired. The remainder of the event was a Stuck benefit, but the March-BMWs were unable to prevent Arnoux and Tambay taking maximum non-graded honours in their Martini-Renaults.

Thruxton saw the débuts of the Abarth-engined Wheatcroft and John Nicholson's March 752 driven by the four-cylinder Chevrolet Vega engine: the former ran its bearings and did not start, while the latter qualified and finished in midfield. Ron Dennis, meanwhile, had already returned the Lancia engines to the Brambilla workshops, borrowing a Hart engine from the

Modus team for Cheever's car instead. This time, March-BMW were fortunate to score a works 1–2, Flammini winning from newcomer Ribeio after Jabouille had closed his Elf-Renault to within 1.05 seconds of the leader before spinning off at the fast Church Corner with three laps to go, caught in turbulence from a backmarker. Tambay nevertheless picked up third place (in front of the Project Four March-Hart) to head the championship table.

The next races, at Vallelunga and the Salzburgring, were victories for the Elf-Renault team. In a reversal of the Thruxton situation, the Italian race saw Flammini close on Jabouille's leading fuel-starved Elf, only for the March driver to crash into a backmarker in his excitement two laps from the flag. The Austrian event was won by Michel Leclere after team leader Jabouille had slowed with falling oil pressure.

Both races had seen the diminutive René Arnoux press ahead in the lead only to suffer engine breakage at Vallelunga and brainfade at the Salzburgring, but the Frenchman's turn came at the following Pau round, where he pressured team mate Tambay into a spin and then staved off the challenges of a cramped Jacques Laffite (guesting in Opert's Chevron-BMW) for a popular win. The March 762s were strangely off the pace on the small street circuit, and the problem — the rear suspension design — was not discovered until near the end of the season, by which time the cars had suffered similar poor performances at Mugello and Nogaro, losing valuable championship points. Pau also saw the F2 début of Canadian Formula Atlantic Champion, Gilles Villeneuve, whose March-Hart pitted after three laps with overheating problems.

Hockenheim and Rouen saw March restore some of the balance, Stuck claiming his second consecutive F2 win at Hockenheim in the space of three months (while Flammini and Ribeiro eliminated each other), and Flammini conquering a hot Rouen once Arnoux's Martini-Renault developed a misfire. The French race was a dramatic affair as Tom Pryce — drafted by Chevron into Opert's BMW-powered car — slid off when well up, Jabouille finished second after keeping one hand on a loose fire extinguisher through Rouen's several fast corners, and Keke Rosberg challenged for third place, only to fall back with broken seat fittings. Another worthy performance came from René Arnoux, who, once fitted with a new sparkbox, rejoined over a lap down to set fastest lap and close on Jabouille's Elf-Renault at the rate of three seconds a lap despite a deflating tyre.

This result brought Flammini up to third place in the championship, in amongst the Renault runners and just a point behind joint leaders Jabouille and Tambay. But this was the closest March-BMW got — for the rest of the season, the race for championship honours was between Jabouille and Arnoux, with Tambay keeping the remaining hopefuls at bay.

Following Mugello, where Jean-Pierre Jabouille beat the Martini-Renaults to the line, Enna witnessed its usual spate of alarming, high-speed accidents, Arnoux rolling his Martini on kerbing at one of the chicanes and Ingo Hoffman writing off his third March of the year when his brakes failed. Project Four continued on their unhappy way — after colliding at 155mph with a flock of birds at Mugello, at Enna Cheever somehow managed to crash the replacement car during the race warm-up. Arnoux took the race honours from Ribeiro once Flammini had spun away his first heat lead and crashed in Heat 2.

Estoril next month saw the début of the Mk19 Martini, featuring rear suspension geometry designed around the Renault engine, and another victory for its driver, René Arnoux. After experiencing handling problems in practice, Jabouille tore round the bumpy Portuguese circuit, his yellow Elf-Renault finally finishing second with half of its driveshaft retaining bolts sheared! The poorly-supported race featured the unusual sight of more Chevrons than Marches on the starting grid.

With Jean-Pierre now only four points behind his French rival, the penultimate round at Nagoro was a thrilling affair. After 16 of the 65 laps the first six cars were covered by two seconds; Jabouille, Arnoux, Leclere, Jarier, Tambay and Laffite scrapping merrily and putting on a fine exhibition of home-grown talent before the French crowd. Following Jabouille's retirement with a broken gearbox and Arnoux's with a dropped valve, Tambay collected his third F2 win at the circuit and the championship remained undecided until the final round, a two-heat affair at Hockenheim.

The event proved a classic tactical confrontation between the Elf and Martini teams. Jabouille claimed pole from Stuck (March-BMW), the Martini-Renaults of Tambay and Arnoux, and teammate Leclere. On the opening lap of Heat One — held on a damp and slippery track — Stuck, who had made a slow start compared to his Renault-engined neighbours, collided with Tambay, sending both out of contention. The championship his, provided he could remain second to Jabouille, René Arnoux nevertheless tried his hardest to force the leading Elf into a mistake, but Jabouille coolly ran out the 20 laps 3.8 seconds to the good, with Leclere third, 6.6 seconds behind Arnoux.

In the break between the heats, the Elf team planned their strategy, which involved Jabouille keeping Arnoux at bay while Leclere took a heat

The French drivers put on a fine scrap for the home crowd at Nogaro – Jabouille (Elf) leads from Arnoux (Martini), Leclere (Elf),Tambay (Martini) and Jarier (Opert Chevron).

Good teamwork by the Elf-Renault équipe saw Jean-Pierre Jabouille claim the championship in his self-designed car.

win, hopefully sufficiently far ahead to snatch second place overall from the Martini driver. Their plans were helped by Arnoux making a particularly poor start: Leclere took over Jabouille's lead on lap 2, and pulled away. A charging Arnoux overcame Jabouille's delaying tactics three laps later, but the yellow Elf remained glued to the Martini's tail, regaining second place on lap 12 and staying there, Leclere's 6.6 seconds lead at the flag being just enough to give his teamleader overall victory and demote Arnoux to third. After 12 races throughout Europe, Jabouille had taken the championship by 1.5 seconds and one point!

1977 – F2 Aperitif

1977 marked the last year of Elf's planned involvement in F2, and Arnoux, driving one of the Elf-sponsored Martini-Renaults, began the season as championship favourite. He would be supported by European Formule Renault Champion, Didier Pironi in another works Mk22, while a customer car was supplied, appropriately, to Giancarlo Martini. Last year's successful Elf-Renaults were purchased by Willi Kauhsen (and the cars renamed accordingly), who had obtained the driving services of Michel Leclere and Klaus Ludwig.

Opposition to the Renault-engined teams was, however, intensified. March produced a streamlined BMW-powered 772P chassis for their drivers Patrick Neve, Alex Ribeiro and Marc Surer, while widebody versions were sold to AFMP (running the new Italian hope Bruno Giacomelli,

who had snatched Scaini sponsorship away from Maurizio Flammini), Euroracing (entering Alberto Colombo and Alessandro Pesenti-Rossi) and Ricardo Zunino amongst others. Ralt produced chassis for Project Four team drivers Eddie Cheever and Ingo Hoffman, using Heine Mader-built BMW engines, and also for the Minardi Scuderia Ferrari-powered project to be driven by Gianfranco Brancatelli and Lamberto Leoni. Chevron too provided Minardi with their B40 chassis for coupling with the new Dino V6, although the Bolton firm's main hopes rested with the semi-works BMW-engined Trivellato car for European F3 Champion Riccardo Patrese and with the Hart-powered customer cars of Guy Edwards and Fred Opert (running Keke Rosberg and American Wink Bancroft). Other B40s were sold to the French Chrysler-engined ROC team led again by veteran Jean-Pierre Jaussaud.

Of the smaller manufacturers, Toj produced a new chassis for American Danny Sullivan, while Boxer and Wheatcroft cars — both Hart-powered — would be driven by Brian Henton and ex-F1 racer Bob Evans respectively. A number of customised Lolas appeared without success during the season, including a Holbay Abarth-engined model which destroyed both powerplants in practice at Silverstone and was never seen again.

It was soon apparent that the Martini-Renaults would not have things all their own way. Arnoux did win the opening Silverstone round ahead of an impressive Ray Mallock (Chevron-Hart), but only after Neve's March, leading

Brian Henton (here leading Leclere's Kauhsen-Renault) took the under-financed Boxer-Hart PR276 to Britain's first F2 victory for four years after a typically spirited drive at Thruxton.

48   *The Martini-Renaults of Didier Pironi and René Arnoux at an overcast Nürburgring.*

comfortably, was forced in with a loose wheel nut; the Belgian finishing third, setting a new F2 lap record in the process, and was immediately offered a F1 drive with Frank Williams. Thruxton witnessed a thrilling fight for the lead once Cheever had to make for the pits in his leading Ralt with a slow puncture. Patrese's Chevron-BMW took up the running under pressure from Leclere's Kauhsen, Henton (Boxer-Hart) and Giacomelli (March-Hart). The latter was the first to retire from the fray with a broken accelerator cable just 12 laps from home, Leclere dropped out on the next tour following a collision with a recovering Cheever, and Patrese's car developed a misfire and then stopped for fresh rubber with just nine laps to go. And so Brian Henton took the Boxer to an unexpected and popular win — the first British F2 success since Roger Williamson's victory at Monza four years earlier.

The two German rounds at Hockenheim (which marked the end of the Boxer's race season because of lack of funds) and the Nürburgring featured graded drivers, Jochen Mass driving a works March-BMW at both venues, Jacques Laffite behind the wheel of an Opert Chevron-Hart at Hockenheim, whilst a Project Four Ralt-BMW was supplied for firstly Hans Stuck and then Clay Regazzoni. On both occasions, outright victory went to Mass's Yardley-sponsored car, while young Eddie Cheever shone once more, retiring his Ralt-BMW when lying second at Hockenheim but retaining runner-up position to the flag on the Eifel track. René Arnoux finished second and fifth in these races to maintain his championship lead, but, by Vallelunga — where he retired and Cheever finished third behind Pironi and a dominant Giacomelli (in the works March following the dissolution of the AFMP setup) — the Italian-domiciled American had closed to within three points of the Frenchman.

Then the 19-year-old's luck ended. At Pau, he was eliminated in someone else's startline shunt: the race was stopped during a heavy rainstorm which sent four cars off the road at the tricky Station Hairpin and was deemed to have finished on the previous lap, giving Martini-Renault a 1–2 result, Arnoux from Pironi. The French équipe suffered handling problems in the next round at Mugello, but Cheever crashed out-lapping a backmarker, and another win for Giacomelli saw the genial Italian briefly attain second place to Arnoux in the championship table.

By Rouen, Ron Dennis's team had identified a wiring error which had affected the performance of Cheever's engine since Vallelunga, and had fitted cockpit-adjustable rear anti-roll bar and brake balance systems. The Ralt annexed pole and ran faultlessly in the race, giving Eddie a

comfortable first F2 win ahead of Patrese's Chevron and Pironi's Martini: Arnoux was involved in yet another startline accident, and was now just two points to the good from his American rival.

The next round at Nogaro resulted in a flag-to-flag victory for the championship leader, Patrese charging hard to finish second. The Italian's performance was particularly commendable given that South-West France was badly affected by floods, stranding the Trivellato team prior to practice and causing Riccardo to manage only a couple of hours' sleep in a damp transporter the night before the race. The next day, Patrese chased Giacomelli furiously until they touched, pressured Cheever into a spin and then closed on Arnoux until he spun the Chevron in front of the pits.

A hot and dusty Enna witnessed a final attempt by Cheever and Patrese to get on championship terms with Arnoux. This was one of the few championship rounds to still retain a two-heat format, and in Heat 1 Patrese led the field until a spin forced him to stop for fresh tyres, handing victory to Cheever 0.3 seconds ahead of the Chevron-Hart of Keke Rosberg (just arriving from a Formula Atlantic win for Fred Opert in Canada), with Arnoux well back after assorted incidents. Heat 2 began badly for Rosberg (getting away 12th); Patrese led again until his rear suspension broke, and then Arnoux overtook Cheever, a determined Rosberg following the Martini-Renault through simultaneously. Cheever, hoping for an overall win, hung on in third but eventually spun off, race honours going to Rosberg, although the moustachioed Finn ceded the heat to Arnoux, who claimed six more points for second overall.

The F2 circus then moved to Misano for the first time, the organisers having lined up Regazzoni and Merzario (Opert Chevron-Harts) and Vittorio Brambilla (Kauhsen-Renault) amongst the regular contestants to lure spectators away from the nearby Adriatic beaches. With Arnoux eliminating himself in a stupid corner-cutting manoeuvre just after the start, the race marked an extraordinary F2 début for 19-year-old ex-kart racer Elio de Angelis. At the wheel of one of the Minardi Ralt-Ferraris, the Italian youngster led the first heat from Merzario and Patrese's Chevrons until the latter punted Merzario off just after half-distance. Then Leoni (Trivellato Chevron-Ferrari) and Cheever (Ralt-BMW) caught de Angelis, Cheever pressing the inexperienced leader into a mistake just two laps from home and going on to take the chequered flag with just a few pounds of air left in a front tyre which had been leaking all the race. De Angelis recovered to finish fourth, behind Leoni and Hoffman (Ralt-BMW). The second heat was less frenetic: Cheever had to

Misano saw a strong one-off performance by Ferrari-engined runners. Eventual winner Lamberto Leoni (Trivellato Chevron-Ferrari Dino B40) leads F2 débutant Elio de Angelis (Minardi Ralt-Ferrari Dino RT1), the Project Four Ralt-BMW RT1s of Cheever and Hoffman and the rest of the field.

defend a 0.7 seconds advantage over Leoni, but the Italian got the better start and went on to win by 3.4 seconds, giving the Ferrari Dino V6 its one and only F2 victory. Cheever was classified second overall from team-mate Hoffman to make it a fine day for Ralt as well.

The cancellation of races at Zolder and the Salzburgring led to a six-week break before the penultimate championship round on the challenging Portuguese circuit of Estoril. René Arnoux had simply to finish ahead of Cheever to be assured of the title. Martini turned up with long wheelbase Mk22s and Pironi gained an easy win in one of them, but behind things were more fraught as a single-minded Cheever caught second man Arnoux in the closing stages, only to be deflected from his task by an equally determined Keke Rosberg, whose attempts to get past the Ralt-BMW enabled Arnoux to stay half a second ahead of both of them at the flag, the championship his. Estoril also marked the F2 débuts of Alain Prost (Kauhsen-Renault), Eje Elgh (Opert Chevron-Hart) and Derek Daly (Guy Edwards Chevron-Hart), the Irishman putting in the best performance by finishing fifth and setting fastest lap.

The 13-race series had produced six dif-ferent maximum points winners, driving six different chassis powered by four different engines. In a season which had featured outstanding and varied competition, René Arnoux and Martini (who were to enter F1 together in 1978) had taken the Championship through consistency rather than the outright superiority which some had forecast at the start of the year.

1978 – Practice Makes Perfect

A foretaste of things to come in 1978 was given at the final 1977 round at the newly re-opened Donington Park race circuit. Bruno Giacomelli totally dominated the event in the development March 782 chassis, taking pole grid position, leading from start to finish and securing fastest lap. By this time (October), the BMW-powered car had already covered 600 miles of development testing with Giacomelli at the wheel. With Elf and Renault now setting their sights exclusively on a Le Mans victory and the F1 title, and BMW's promising Marc Surer and Manfred Winkelhock joining Giacomelli at March, the Bicester firm were clearly going all out to re-establish their supremacy in F2.

Up against the works Marches would be Ron

Dennis's Project Four operation, retaining Eddie Cheever and Ingo Hoffman but running March-BMWs now under the auspices of the BMW Challenge Team; Guy Edwards' ICI Racing Chevron-Harts for Derek Daly and various 'star' guests; Fred Opert's similar Chevrons for Keke Rosberg, Eje Elgh and Dutchman Boy Hayje; Rad Dougall's Toleman Group March-BMW; the private March-Harts of Brian Henton, Alex Ribeiro and Alberto Colombo; European F3 Champion Piercarlo Ghinzani in a Pavanello-run March-BMW; Piero Necchi, retaining Pirelli radial tyres and using Osella-tuned BMWs in his March chassis; and several times world motorcycle champion Giacomo Agostini in a Trivellato Chevron-Ferrari. Ralt were not in a position to pursue a F2 effort this season, but a tiny French constructor, Automobiles Gonfarennaise Sportives, would enter a single AGS-BMW for their Formule Super Renault driver Richard Dallest.

Before the season had even started, Chevron Cars were knocked sideways by the death of designer and founder Derek Bennett. The B42 chassis — developed from last year's model — proved disappointingly uncompetitive at the opening Thruxton round with a marked reluctance to turn into corners. The various Chevron runners turned their attention to ironing these problems out, and by the end of the season had notched up three wins to their credit.

Two of these came at consecutive rounds at Mugello and Vallelunga and involved Derek Daly, of the ICI Racing team. Daly got off to a good start at the Tuscan circuit, and thereafter only had to overcome a half-distance challenge from Marc Surer (March-BMW) and an emptying on-board fire extinguisher to take the chequered flag. Vallelunga was a trickier proposition, Daly leading from Necchi's Pirelli-shod March after a number of startline shunts had sidelined other contenders, until, on lap 18, gear selection problems leaving the hairpin saw Giacomelli's March nip ahead. The works combination established a 10-second lead but, 10 laps from home, slowed as hay over the radiators caused the oil temperature to soar. The ICI Chevron itself had sprung a small oil leak, but the gap between the two cars steadily narrowed and, when one of the March's pistons seized on the last lap, Daly was able to get by and win by a second.

The other Chevron victory came three weeks later at a chilly Donington. With the championship round run as two 40-lap heats, Heat 1 was dominated by the March-Hart of local man Brian Henton until a pressure gauge leak forced him to the pits for a change of overalls! Behind, a furious scrap was waged between Giacomelli's March, Rosberg's Chevron-Hart and Necchi's March, increasing its speed as its Pirellis gradually warmed. Rosberg successfully out-braked the March team leader into the chicane, while Necchi challenged at Redgate, sending Bruno somersaulting off and damaging the Astra car's handling

Keke Rosberg (Opert Chevron-Hart B42) fending off the challenge of Piero Necchi's Pirelli-shod Astra March-BMW 782 at Donington.

in the process. Nevertheless, the Italian March continued to close on Rosberg, who held off his challenger by just half a second at the flag. Track temperatures were even colder for the second heat, Necchi dropping down to ninth before his Pirellis began to grip and took him up to fifth. Rosberg — his eye on an overall win — settled for fourth in the heat behind Surer, Hoffman and Henton, which was good enough for the race honours.

Keke might well have enjoyed more successes during the season were it not for a number of niggling problems, misfortune and other racing commitments which prevented him from entering each round. The nearest he came to another win was at the Nürburgring, where, after cooking his clutch on the line and getting away ninth, he took the Chevron up to a fierce duel for the lead with Alex Ribeiro (March-Hart) and Eddie Cheever (March-BMW). Ribeiro was inspired that day, the Brazilian entering the last corner first to beat the Finn by a car-length, with Cheever third.

The rest of the season belonged to March-BMW, and particularly to the chubby Bruno Giacomelli, who won all of the remaining eight races. By the start of the season, the front radiatored 782 had covered 2000 testing miles — preparation which resulted in an amazingly fast and reliable machine. The first two races brought works 1—2s, Surer backing up Giacomelli, and a similar result at the ninth round at Nogaro meant the Italian teamleader had the opportunity to be acclaimed champion on homeground at Enna. Giacomelli duly won, despite a last-lap puncture, from a battling Cheever (his BMW about to blow) and Daly, whose Chevron finished with a tyre down to canvas. The last two races ended the season as it began — two more 1—2s for Giacomelli and Surer, with Winkelhock finishing third at the final Hockenheim round to put the seal on March's

and BMW's success. Giacomelli (the first Italian to win the European Championship) and Surer had ended up well clear of the remaining drivers in the table.

F1 drivers continued to appear intermittently in F2 with varying degrees of success. Patrick Tambay, in one of the ICI Chevrons, almost beat Giacomelli at Pau, the Frenchman leading comfortably until the oil pressure light came on 13 laps from the end and he slowed to save the engine: his lead was so substantial he could bear the loss of two seconds a lap, but his engine cried enough on the final circuit and that was that. Jean-Pierre Jarier appeared in a March-BMW on four occasions, but was generally lacklustre, and Jochen Mass crashed his Chevron on his only appearance at Thruxton. Jacques Laffite experienced mixed fortunes in his F2 showings, but Merzario and Regazzoni showed strongly in their few appearances. F2 regulars to make an impression included Geoff Lees, Rad Dougall, Eje Elgh and Ricardo Zunino, while the enterprising Nova team came over from Japan to contest two championship events using Bridgestone tyres, driver Kazuyoshi Hoshino showing particularly well at Donington.

In fact, the season marked the beginnings of a small tyre war. Once Piero Necchi had achieved second fastest practice time at Vallelunga on Pirellis, Goodyear began issuing quicker rubber to a selection of their runners. Elio de Angelis fitted American M&H tyres to his ICI Chevron at Misano and finished in the top three.

Among the season's disappointments were Giacomo Agostini, who usually failed to qualify for the races; the heavy Ferrari V6; Michel Leclere (who was unable to qualify Rosberg's Chevron at Rouen); and the SuperVee-based Maco-BMW which only appeared in practice at the April Hockenheim meeting.

1978 marked a return to March superiority in the Formula, works teamleader Bruno Giacomelli taking the March-BMW 782 to eight race wins and the European Championship.

1979 – Two Laps From Victory

After the successes of 1978, March expanded their works operation to run no less than seven cars in the 1979 European Championship. Following his year playing second fiddle to Bruno Giacomelli, Swiss Marc Surer would lead the BMW Polifac Junior Team, with Guiseppe 'Beppe' Gabbiani and Ricardo Zunino as back-up. A further factory entry, fitted with a Heine Mader-prepared BMW engine, would be driven by Teo Fabi, who had run away with the New Zealand Formula Pacific title during the winter. In addition, Project Four would this season be masterminding the ICI Racing March-BMWs of Derek Daly and Stephen South, and finally Argentine Juan Traverso would be at the wheel of a March-Hart entrusted to Bob Salisbury. All cars would run on Goodyear rubber.

The main opposition to this March onslaught would seem to come from Osella, the Toleman Group (entering the works Ralts) and Chevron. The Italian engine specialist would be running his own chassis, admittedly a four-year-old design, but with Eddie Cheever at the wheel and an exclusive contract with Pirelli Tyres. Toleman had struck up a deal with Brian Hart to supply his all-alloy 420R motor for their Ralt chassis and had engaged Brian Henton to join Rad Dougall as team driver. Chevron had called in Tony Southgate to redesign the B42 as a ground-effects car; the works B48 entry for American Bobby Rahal would be Hart-powered as well.

With Lotus having dominated F1 the previous season with their revolutionary 79 'wing-car', ground effect design was clearly the way to go, and March therefore produced an all-new 792 with the engine as a stressed member, inboard suspension, and a slim monocoque with side venturis.

Of the privateers, Siegfried Stohr and Huub Rothengatter would run Chevrons, fitted with BMW and Hart engines respectively; Tim Schenken and Howden Ganley would enter a March-BMW for Eje Elgh under their Tiga banner; Alberto Colombo would also use Pirelli rubber on his March-BMW; and Theodore Racing had reached agreement with BP to run Derek Warwick in a March-Hart. Small constructors would continue to be represented by AGS (running last year's car for Alain Couderc), hillclimb specialists Pilbeam (their Hart-engined MP42 model to be driven by Patrick Neve), Maurer (Armin Hahne at the wheel), and the V6-powered AMS for Piero Necchi.

A combination of factors produced one of the most exciting F2 seasons ever, the championship now comprising a compact dozen races held between March and August.

Firstly, Pirelli's wet-weather product was far superior to Goodyear's and solid preparation before the start of the season saw the overweight Osella achieve a good standard of reliability. The opening championship round at Silverstone was subjected to heavy rain, the race having to be stopped at one point when the Woodcote chicane became blocked with crashed vehicles. At the restart, Cheever again took the lead but came under heavy pressure from Henton's Ralt (completed just days before the race) and Daly's March. Henton managed to get past, only to spin with gear selection problems, while a further spin by Daly as he attempted to overtake the orange Osella dropped the Irishman 12 seconds behind. With the track drying, Daly recovered to take the lead eight laps from home, but gear linkage problems on the ICI March meant that the two cars entered the last lap nose-to-tail. At Maggots, Cheever drew alongside, but the March — with its superior braking — kept the lead through Becketts and it wasn't until Hangar Straight that the Osella could hit the front once more, Daly hanging on and only 0.33 seconds separating them at the finish.

Pau was also run in heavy rain, and again Cheever splashed his way round to the chequered flag, despite damaging the Beta-sponsored Osella's suspension in a coming-together with early leader Derek Daly. A hastily-arranged fixture at Zandvoort saw dry weather, but the track's abrasive surface suited the Pirellis more than the opposition and brought a third trouble-free win for the Italian team. As the circus gathered for the last championship round at Donington, Cheever had amassed 32 points to hold joint runner-up position with a chance at the title.

The second factor centred on development problems with the March 792 chassis: at Silverstone, it was discovered that the aerodynamics generated far too much downforce, the cars being virtually sucked into the track. Drivers also complained of the overweight 792's unpredictability.

This meant that the pre-season favourite for the championship, Marc Surer, had a far from easy time, the gritty Swiss winning just two rounds, at the Nürburgring (where he successfully risked starting with slick tyres on a circuit wet over half its 14-mile length) and Vallelunga. Other finishes in the points in the latter half of the season, as the 792 improved, meant that Surer went to Donington in exactly the same position as Cheever.

The final factor was the late production of the Toleman Group Ralts and the consequent problems in racing cars straight out of the box. Early in the season when only one Ralt was ready and proving problematic, both Henton and Dougall reverted to their previous year's Marches (Dougall, in fact, won at Thruxton in his 782, while

Eddie Cheever (Osella-BMW FA2/79) under pressure from Brian Henton's newly-completed Toleman Ralt-Hart RT2 during the exciting Silverstone round.

54   *Marc Surer's factory March-BMW 792 ahead of Rad Dougall's Toleman March-Hart 782 at Vallelunga.*

Brian Henton (Toleman Ralt-Hart RT2) seemed all set to clinch the European Championship at the final Donington round, only to spin off the track with brake problems just two laps from home.

Henton came second at the Nürburgring in his similar car), and Toleman were grateful for the five-week mid-season gap which enabled their development engineer Rory Byrne to alter venturi profiles and shock absorber ratings and to fit new sidepods, springs, roll-bars, engine mountings and a rear wing arrangement, shedding 10lb weight at the same time. After this, they were able to add to Henton's earlier win at Mugello with further victories by Brian at Enna and Misano. Unfortunately, the Enna result was the basis of a dispute lasting several months, runner-up Eje Elgh's Tiga team protesting that the Ralt should have been disqualified after taking to an escape road to avoid a first-corner melée and then not stopping before rejoining the track. With the protest backed by the race organisers, Henton arrived at Donington as the championship leader on 33 points – only one point ahead of Surer and Cheever.

In practice, March drivers Derek Daly and Teo Fabi annexed the front row of the grid – with Henton next up despite two practice crashes. Surer had had a nasty run-off at Starkey's Bridge, necessitating a medical check-up, but would start alongside the Englishman, whilst Cheever was only tenth fastest in a lightweight Osella.

An on-form Daly soon took the lead of the race from Fabi and shot off into the distance, chased by Henton, while Surer held third spot from Stephen South's ICI March. As the race entered its closing stages, so the leading runners closed on each other, Henton right behind Daly now, and Surer a few seconds back, making up

ground amidst the race traffic. Then – just over two laps away from the flag – the Ralt's front brakes failed approaching the Old Hairpin and the car suddenly slewed round off the track and onto the grass; by the time Henton could recover, both Surer and South had gone past, and a stunned crowd suddenly found 'Superhen' deposed and Marc Surer proclaimed champion – a title subsequently confirmed by the FIA Appeal Court some weeks later, when the Enna disqualification was upheld.

As the dust settled from a most hard-fought season, so other performances could be noted. Derek Daly's Donington win netted him third place in the championship ahead of Cheever, and he might well have taken the title himself had it not been for some prior F1 commitments at the start of the season. Stephen South, Daly's team mate, claimed a victory at Hockenheim and proved extremely rapid, and Teo Fabi was another to show considerable promise. Siegfried Stohr managed a couple of good results in his Chevron-BMW, but no other marques were really in contention. British F3 Champion Stefan Johansson put on a terrific performance in a works March at Donington, whilst Keke Rosberg (sitting in for Daly) dominated the April Hockenheim event and lapped the Nürburgring just outside the outright F1 lap record before his car was written off when the throttle jammed open.

1980 – Winning for Britain
The most exciting winter news in Britain prior to the 1980 season (which would again feature a

Beginning as they meant to continue. . . the Toleman-Hart TG280s of Derek Warwick and Brian Henton on their way to a 1–2 result at Thruxton. Thackwell's March-BMW 802 follows.

56

dozen races in England, Germany, Italy, France, Belgium and Holland) was that the Toleman Group had constructed their own F2 car, the TG280, fitted with Hart engine and running on Pirelli radials, and had reached agreement with BP for an all-British pairing of Stephen South and Derek Warwick as drivers. Controversy arose just before the start of the season, when South was dismissed for missing a day's development testing in favour of a McLaren F1 test drive: his replacement was none other than Brian Henton, who, incredibly, had no other drive lined up for 1980. (Poor South ended up CanAm racing instead, only to lose a leg in a bad crash later in the year.) Customer Tolemans were built for Siegfried Stohr and Huub Rothengater (both entries to be prepared by Alan Docking) and for Alberto Colombo.

March also produced a neat, straightforward ground-effect chassis in the 802 and continued their collaboration with BMW and with Goodyear tyres. This year, the works team would be confined to three drivers — Teo Fabi, Manfred Winklehock and Alan Jones's F3 protégé Mike Thackwell — whilst customer cars would be run by Project Four for Andrea de Cesaris and Chico Serra, and a number of Marches of earlier vintage would appear.

Only one Ralt was ordered (for Rad Dougall) in time for the start of the championship series, but later Ron Tauranac announced he would be constructing another new chassis to fit a works-prepared Honda V6 engine and race it from mid-season: the driver would be Nigel Mansell.

A number of other developments promised a particularly interesting year. AGS produced a new model, the wide track JH17, for Richard Dallest to campaign once more. Maurer (having failed to qualify for most of the 1979 races) acquired the services of a number of ex-Chevron staff, the Bolton firm having ceased trading, as well as Eje Elgh and the young Austrian hope Markus Höttinger. The Swedish driver also helped develop the Tiga F280, to be raced by BMW protégé Hans-Georg Bürger. The Italian Minardi team also decided to build their own car this season, running on Pirelli tyres and driven by Argentine Angel Guerra, whilst ex-F1 driver Arturo Merzario produced the primitive Merzario M1 for himself and Guido Dacco (although Dacco's ride was soon transferred to Piero Necchi).

Tyres played an important part in the outcome of the season. Most of Toleman's development was based upon their Pirelli tyres, and severe pre-season understeer was eliminated once Rory Byrne had paid a personal visit to the firm's Milan factory to plead for stiffer construction rubber. In fact, Pirelli produced new constructions and compounds throughout the season for Henton

and Byrne to evaluate — and also provided qualifying tyres, which Goodyear refrained from doing. The Goodyear runners, meanwhile, all complained of a lack of grip and met with a slow response from the company, who were more concerned with regaining the F1 World Championship.

Skirts were banned on F2 cars this year, but Toleman gained another advantage over their rivals by Rory Byrne's individual interpretation of the regulation, which prompted him to drop the driver's seat through the monocoque, keeping the bottom of the bodywork to within a centimetre of the seat's underside and thereby assisting the Toleman's side-pods to touch the road under braking and create the same partial vacuum as sliding skirts had generated previously. The arrangement was discovered at Vallelunga and declared legal, and March could only follow suit.

With an excellent reliability record as well, the BP-liveried Toleman-Harts totally dominated the championship. From 11 starts, Derek Warwick managed one win, three second places, three thirds and a fourth, while a masterly Brian Henton scored three wins, five second places and a third to claim the title which had eluded him in 1979 by a huge 19-point margin from his team mate. Typical of the thinking behind Brian's driving this year was his performance at a hot Vallelunga. Second fastest to Warwick in practice, Henton was initially involved in a busy leading group comprising the two Tolemans and the Marches of Fabi, de Cesaris and Thackwell. Just as it seemed leader Fabi might break away, 'Superhen' passed his team mate for second, hung onto the back of the Roloil-sponsored March and adjusted his roll bar, the car moving from oversteer to understeer. After 23 laps, Fabi oversteered just slightly too much through the circuit's s-bends and the yellow and white Toleman was through, its driver immediately concentrating on establishing a small lead and then adjusting the car's balance to compensate for a badly worn left tyre. In the meantime, de Cesaris and Warwick had managed to further demote Fabi and began closing on the leader, but, mindful of his shredding tyre, Brian just increased his pace a fraction to win by 4.4 seconds.

Down in 13th position at the end of practice at the Nürburgring, but with new tyres fitted for the race, Henton was up to seventh by the end of the first lap and three laps later had forged through to second behind Fabi (March-BMW) — a position he maintained until the end. Derek Warwick, despite disliking the circuit, did just as well to rise from 14th to third. Later in the season, at Zolder, it was Warwick who, spinning down to 23rd on the third lap, put in the drive of the year by storming back to fourth place: at this race,

Toleman took a 1-2-3-4 (Rothengatter-Stohr-Henton-Warwick) to add to their three 1-2s at Thruxton, Mugello and Enna (where Stohr won after the engine on Gabbiani's leading Maurer blew four laps from the flag).

Teo Fabi finished third in the championship table four points down on Warwick, the March team-leader winning all three German rounds in scintillating fashion but suffering a spate of engine failures in mid-season.

There were other names too to conjure with for the future. New Zealander Mike Thackwell displayed immense natural ability, carving his way from last to second at the April Hockenheim and setting fastest lap before the engine blew, putting on a similar performance at the Núrburgring and nearly winning Zandvoort after an astonishing practice run in the rain. 21-year-old Andrea de Cesaris established himself as the fastest driver in F2, albeit prone to accidents, and persuaded Marlboro to secure him a F1 drive for 1981. His Project Four March won at Misano after crashing out of the lead six laps from home at Zandvoort. The AGS — an also-ran in dry conditions — proved ideally suited to wet races, and Richard Dallest had a superb season with the shoestring-financed team, the only driver to lap the Nürburgring in under nine minutes and winner at Pau and Zandvoort. Maurers, too, showed more promise than before, although they still suffered from poor reliability and had a great deal of misfortune besides. Teamleader Eje Elgh missed a large chunk of the season after breaking an arm testing the Tiga, whilst Markus Höttinger was killed by an errant wheel in an accident at the April Hockenheim. Maurer had to resort to replacement

drivers as a result, but nevertheless both Patrick Gaillard and Beppe Gabbiani impressed, leading at Pau and Enna respectively until their machinery let them down.

Tiga were also touched by tragedy when Hans-Georg Bürger (who had shown genuine promise whilst acclimatising to the one-off car) crashed fatally at Zandvoort's fifth-gear Scheivlak corner: the team subsequently withdrew from the Formula.

At the September Hockenheim meeting the two revamped Ralt-Hondas of Nigel Mansell and Geoff Lees were most impressive. With modified cylinder heads and an exhaust system taken out of the venturi, they were second and fourth to Fabi's pole in practice, but both got ahead of the March into the first corner, the three cars pulling away in a class of their own (the championship-winning Tolemans were absent on this occasion). Behind Lees, Mansell and Fabi fought for second place until the lead Ralt spun on oil and suddenly the positions were reversed! Within three laps, Lees (employing a higher top gear than the others) was back in front, and then Fabi began to drop back with severe oversteer. The Ralts looked set for an impressive 1-2 victory, but first Lees halted with a punctured wheel off the rim and then — with three laps remaining — Mansell began to run out of fuel and Fabi had soon charged past for a swansong win for sponsors ICI. Nevertheless, the Ralt-Hondas were clearly going to be a force to be reckoned with in the coming season.

1981 — Return of the Rising Sun
The Anglo-Japanese project's serious intentions were underlined during the 'off-season' when

Teo Fabi (March-BMW 802) managed a number of impressive showings during the season, including a win at the Nürburgring.

The tiny AGS équip produced a BMW-engined chassis which performed marvellously in wet conditions. Here, Richard Dallest holds the lead at Zandvoort.

Honda produced 20 of their 330bhp iron-block V6 engines (redesigned so as not to interfere with the venturi diffuser system) and Ralt refined the aerodynamics of the RH6 and announced Geoff Lees and Mike Thackwell as drivers.

Toleman were taking their 1980 F2 team into F1 this year, leaving Lola to manufacture replicas of the successful TG280. The works-assisted Lola-built T850s were entrusted to the Docking-Spitzley operation, running Stefan Johansson and Kenneth Acheson, both fresh from British F3. Two more of these expensive cars were sold to privateers Fredy Schnarwiler and Guido Pardini, who opted to use BMW engines rather than the Hart motors for which the chassis were designed. The original TG280s would be campaigned by Jim Crawford, Carlo Rossi and Jo Gartner amongst others.

March were determined to get back on terms with their 812 model — a logical development of last year's car — for European F3 graduates Corrado Fabi and Thierry Boutsen and BMW saloon car protégé Christian Danner. Fabi and Danner would run the latest Paul Rosche BMW M12 engine, while Boutsen would use a Heine Mader version of the German four-cylinder. Privateer entries would come from Onyx Racing (for Riccardo Paletti), Arturo Merzario (two cars for himself and Pierro Necchi) and Markus Hotz, running an 812 on a rent-a-drive basis.

The Maurer challenge looked stronger than ever this year, the team moving to the old Chevron factory at Bolton and Gustav Brunner producing a beautiful, high-technology car for Eje Elgh and Colomban Roberto Guerrero, powered this year by Heine Mader units. Minardi, too, came up with an improved chassis (for European F3 Champion Michele Alboreto and Venezuelan 350cc World Motorcycle Champion Johnny Cecotto), able to accept Mader BMW or Ferrari V6 engines. Finally, AGS would enter a sleek JH18 chassis for Richard Dallest, keeping the successful JH17 on hand in case of wet weather.

The F2 calendar was much the same as last year, except that the Dutch fixture had been replaced with an event at Mantorp Park, Sweden, and the Belgian round would take place on the newly-reopened Spa Francorchamps circuit.

Goodyear having withdrawn their support, the season began with most teams either on Pirelli or M&H rubber, with Japanese Dunlops used on occasions. The Silverstone curtain-raiser almost saw a freak win by Swiss privateer Jürg Lienhard, who kept going on wet tyres whilst others made pit stops for changes of rubberwear, but eventually his March-BMW succumbed with a flat battery and victory went instead to Mike Thackwell's Ralt-Honda. The Docking-Spitzley Tolemans were uncompetitive at the British round, having only just been delivered from Lola, but, a

59

week later at Hockenheim, Stefan Johanssan charged his way up from 13th on the grid to just behind third-place man Manfred Winkelhock (Schäfer Ralt-BMW). When the leading Ralt-Hondas hit problems just before the end, these two enjoyed a fine scrap for first place: the German led round the final lap until Johansson made a surprise attack at the Sachskurve – passing on the outside, rather than the usual inside line – to win by just over a second.

By now, most of the Pirelli runners were complaining of lack of durability from the Italian slicks, while the company's harder rubber simply did not grip at all, and so it was not surprising that both Boutsen's March and the Ralts had switched to Japanese tyre manufacturers Bridgestone by the time of the third round at Thruxton. European Championship leader Mike Thackwell crashed his Ralt badly during practice on the Hampshire circuit, the New Zealander being cut out of the wrecked car with a broken heel and toe. In the actual race, the Dunlop-shod Horag March-BMW of guest driver Marc Surer led until lap 33, but first the Maurer-BMW of Guerrero got by and then Eje Elgh's similar car, and, with four laps to go, the white March parked with a blown engine, leaving third to Paletti's Onyx model. The Maurers had been accused of running with sliding skirts in practice, and after the race Elgh's car was disqualified as the scrutineers deemed one of the wing end plates to be too high, although following an appeal the Swede was reinstated in the results at the end of the season. Poleman and early leader had been Thierry Boutsen (March-BMW), who dominated the next race at the Nürburgring, leading from start to finish and establishing a new F2 lap record on his Bridgestone race tyres. This result prompted a mini tyre war, Pirelli defending their reputation by providing quicker rubber to selected runners.

Runner-up once more at the Nürburgring, Eje Elgh (Maurer-BMW) was never headed at the fast and twisty Vallelunga circuit, becoming the fifth winner in five races and moving to the top of the championship table as a result. Fellow-Swede Johansson shadowed the black car for most of the way, but gearbox problems caused the Toleman driver to settle for second place.

Underlining the competitiveness of the season, the following two races produced two more new racewinners! At Pau, it was Geoff Lees who took the lead once Alboreto's Minardi and Acheson's Toleman had collided (the Ulsterman suffering a badly broken leg as a result). With Boutsen's March close behind, a misunderstood pit signal almost caused Lees to cede victory near the finish, the Ralt-Honda slowing at the end of the penultimate lap, but he held on to win by half a second. At Mugello, twenty-year-old Corrado Fabi

(March-BMW) did well to nurse his deteriorating Pirellis to a win from Lees' Ralt-Honda.

With Pirelli's support to the category deteriorating further as the company expanded its involvement in F1, Bridgestone supremacy continued with Thierry Boutsen taking his second win of the year at Enna. The similarly-shod Ralt-Hondas were less fortunate, both Lees and Thackwell (now without the crutches he had used away from his car at Mugello and Pau) going out of contention with 160mph tyre blowouts!

Now that the Honda V6s had been revised with Lucas fuel injection and altered heads, however, so Lees was eager to show his true worth, the Englishman hurling his car to unchallenged victories at a misty Spa and sunny Donington, with the Marches of Boutsen and Fabi respective runners-up. Going to Misano, the penultimate championship round, Geoff enjoyed a six-point lead over Thierry Boutsen, who looked likely to close the gap after a pole position time in practice. The Belgian, however, could only stay in front of Lees for the first four laps of the race and then fell back, his March-BMW jumping out of fourth gear. Team mate Fabi was next to challenge the Ralt-Honda, only to spin out when his engine expired. Then Michele Alboreto, driving superbly and making the most of his Minardi's good roadholding, closed the gap and hit the front shortly after half-distance, Lees staying glued to his tail. With 14 laps remaining, gearbox troubles began afflicting the Ralt, while championship rival Boutsen lost fourth gear completely and dropped to sixth and then eighth and out of the reckoning. The Italians were overjoyed with Alberto's home victory but Ralt, Honda and Bridgestone were happier still, Lees holding his car in second and third gears to finish in second place and claim the championship. Mike Thackwell was pleased with his result also, nipping past Roberto Guerrero's sick Maurer for third place just before the flag.

The last championship race was at Mantorp Park, Sweden (hosting its first F2 event since 1974), and provided a further popular home win for Stefan Johansson (Toleman-Hart), who passed Lees on lap 18 and then was never headed. Behind the champion, making it a good day for Docking-Spitzley, came an exhausted but determined Kenny Acheson (on Avon tyres), back in the cockpit for the first time since Pau. Boutsen finished fourth to claim second place in the championship from Elgh.

Other drivers who impressed on occasions were Manfred Winkelhock, who only did five races but proved unnervingly fast; Johnny Cecotto, whose driving improved remarkably once he left the Minardi team for Markus Hotz's March set-up; the poorly-financed Huub Rothengatter, who took second place in Lienhard's March at Enna; Jim

With a revised Honda V6 engine, the Ralt RH6s came good in the latter half of the season, Geoff Lees claiming the championship with wins at Spa and Donington.

Michele Alboreto produced several strong drives in the Minardi-BMW FLY 281, culminating in a win at Misano.

Crawford, who showed promisingly before losing out once the tyre war got underway; and Jo Gartner, who drove well at Spa in his own Toleman-BMW, only to join Merzario (replacing the sacked Piero Necchi) and lose his way. AGS and Richard Dallest were never front-runners following the Frenchman's concussion in a big accident at Silverstone, Riccardo Paletti began promisingly but lost interest, and the Ferrari and Swindon BDX engines used on occasion respectively by Minardi and Ray Mallock (Ralt) proved uncompetitive.

1982 – A Classic Year

Sensational news at the end of 1981 was that leading March personnel John Wickham and Gordon Coppuck were leaving the Bicester concern to set up their own company, Spirit Racing, which would construct a F2 chassis for 1982 – the first to be tailor-made for the Honda engine. With backing from Marlboro, and a Bridgestone tyre contract, the team would run cars for Stefan Johansson and Thierry Boutsen. A lengthy pre-season test programme produced some daunting times to rattle the opposition.

The Spirit project depleted the resources of the Ralt operation, but nevertheless Ron Tauranac rose to the challenge, completing a purpose-built, honeycomb chassis just in time for the start of the season. Honda engines (with the fuel pump and filter moved inside the tank) and Bridgestone tyres were retained, and Casio sponsorship enabled Tauranac to employ Kenny Acheson and British F3 champion Jonathan Palmer as drivers.

March retained the customer car approach, although the 822 featured horizontal honeycomb beams supporting the faithful BMW engine, while a huge one-piece underbody assisted the airflow underneath the works cars. Development of the new monocoque was carried out by Christian Danner, the March team being led by Corrado Fabi with Johnny Cecotto as number two. Although unable to develop their engine further because of their demanding F1 turbo project, BMW were able to persuade Michelin to exclusively supply radial tyres to their F2 runners. Among the March privateers this year would be Markus Hotz's Horag Racing (running Mike Thackwell – dropped by Ralt partly on grounds of unfitness following his 1981 accident – on a shoestring operation) and Arturo Merzario (using Pirelli sportscar tyres and with Richard Dallest and Jo Gartner on the driving

61

Revelation of the season was Stefan Bellof and the Maurer-BMW MM82, the young German making his mark by winning his first two F2 races.

strength), while Tetsu Ikuzawa planned to run Spirit's test March 812 with a Honda engine for Japanese F2 Champion Satoru Nakajima.

Gustav Brunner tidied up last year's Maurer chassis (the MM82 now using carbon-fibre as well as honeycomb), retained the controversial skirts and also introduced a dual-spring locking device (operable from the cockpit) to improve down-force still further. The works cars would run on Michelin rubber, having agreed with BMW to run twice German Formula Ford Champion Stefan Bellof, and would use the short-stroke BMW engines of Lichtenstein engine-builder Max Heidegger. Beppe Gabbiani and Peter Schindler were the other team drivers while further MM82s were purchased by Bertram Schäfer (using Avon tyres) for Frank Jelinski and Austrian 'Pierre Chauvet'.

Minardi continued with a rebodied version of their 1981 chassis for Italian newcomers Alessandro Nannini and Paolo Barilla: Guido Dacco would drive a two-year-old Minardi for Vittorio Brambilla. AGS also placed their faith in F2 débutants, providing two cars this year for French F3 Champion Philippe Streiff and Pascal Fabré.

There would be no works-assisted Tolemans in the Formula this season, but the Docking-Spitzley team remained faithful to the marque, revising the suspension and bodywork on their Toleman-Harts and entering Thierry Tassin and Carlo Rossi, albeit with the handicap of no engine or tyre contracts. Alberto Colombo's San Remo Tolemans were also retained, now featuring

Heidegger engines, with Roberto del Castello as lead driver.

Pre-season favourite for the championship was Stefan Johansson, widely acknowledged as the Formula's best racer, but, despite taking five pole positions in the Spirit-Honda and leading four races, the Swede had a terrible year, winning never and finishing in the points on only four occasions as his machinery was plagued with both petty problems and incompatibility with a wide range of Bridgestone tyres. Ralt also suffered from the quick-wearing Japanese rubber, while accident damage to the team's cars at the opening Silverstone and Hockenheim rounds seriously delayed their development programme. At mid-season, the team confused itself trying to apply dual rate springs to the skirts, and further accidents reduced their effort to just one car and driver for the last race. Best performances were Acheson's second at Thruxton and Palmer's third at Donington (after leading the race initially), but the combination never looked like strong contenders for championship honours.

Talking-point of the year was young Stefan Bellof, who became the only driver ever to win his first two F2 races. At a predictably showery Silverstone, the 24-year-old German began from ninth on the grid, but wisely conserved his equipment to take his Maurer past Tassin's Toleman (suffering fuel feed problems) for a win just three laps from home: Tassin was later disqualified, his car failing to pass the ruling that skirts should be no less than 4cm above the ground, second place being awarded to Nakajima's March-Honda. Two weeks later at Hockenheim, a confident pole-positioned Bellof charged away from the field at a second a lap for an easy second victory. Thereafter, Stefan's inexperience showed and the Maurer team deteriorated into a series of internal disputes, although the German continued to impress in terms of sheer speed with five fastest laps to his credit.

The championship, then, became a three-cornered fight between Spirit's Thierry Boutsen and March team mates Corrado Fabi and Johnny Cecotto.

Boutsen's first win came at the Nürburgring in April, despite the fact he found his Spirit-Honda almost undriveable on previously unused Bridgestone tyres and he was challenged all the way to the flag. First of all, poleman and fellow-Belgian Thierry Tassin disputed the lead with him until the Toleman dropped back with a broken rear anti-roll bar. Then Boutsen sent a pressing Bellof onto the grass, the rapid Maurer then returning to the pits with blistered rear tyres. Finally, Corrado Fabi moved up to tail the Spirit for the final six laps. Though his March was quicker through the slow corners and he damaged its fin against one of Boutsen's rear tyres he was unable to get by, finishing 0.17 seconds behind at the flag.

Spa in June provided possibly the worst conditions in which a F2 championship race had ever been conducted, the shortened affair taking place amid heavy rain and mist, several cars leaving the road and a number of drivers getting lost in the spray! The two Spirits made the most of their excellent wet rubber, and, once Johansson's engine had cut out, Boutsen sailed to a 23-second

home victory from Cecotto – with Mike Thackwell third, having made three of the six passing manoeuvres seen in the entire race! By the time the circus arrived at Enna in August, Thierry needed a win to retain a chance of the championship in the final round at Misano. The Spirit-Honda led away from pole position, only for a charging Bellof to snatch first place at half-distance: Boutsen retaliated, Bellof counter-attacked, and then Boutsen took advantage of a mistake by the German at the last chicane and pressed determinedly ahead to take the chequered flag.

Johnny Cecotto attained his first F2 win at Thruxton. The abrasive surface took its toll on tyres, and the Venezuelan, running fourth, dropped to fourteenth after a pit-stop for fresh rubber. Charging back through the field the March-BMW took the lead three laps from the end after threading through an excellent scrap between Acheson and Boutsen. At Pau, the former motorbike racer inherited victory once Boutsen's Spirit slowed with dirt in the throttle slides, and the Venezuelan took the championship lead with another win in Sweden when Corrado Fabi hesitated in lapping a back-marker, the resultant collision losing him the race.

Fabi, prior to Misano, had won four races to his rival's three, yet had the hardest task of all to win the championship, Boutsen and Cecotto having achieved more consistent placings in the points. The smooth-driving 21-year-old's first success came at Mugello, his March sprinting through to the front from 12th place on the grid to head Cecotto home in a works 1-2 result. The following week's race at Vallelunga was dominated by the little Italian, and at Hockenheim

Thierry Boutsen takes his Spirit-Honda 201 to victory at a waterlogged Spa.

Johnny Cecotto and Corrado Fabi enjoyed a friendly rivalry all season in their works March-BMW 822s, the Italian (following here at Mantorp) just pipping his team-mate for the championship.

and Donington in June Fabi really charged in the closing stages, demoting the Maurers of Bellof and Gabbiani three laps from home on the German circuit and keeping Cecotto at bay by half a second in the English round.

For the final race at Misano, Cecotto led the championship with 56 points against Boutsen's 50 and Fabi's 48. As drivers could only count their best nine performances from the 13 races, both Boutsen and Fabi would have to go for an outright win and hope that Cecotto finished no higher than third (in Boutsen's case) or fourth (in Fabi's).

Practice was dry, with Fabi recording fastest time and Boutsen and Cecotto back in fourth and eighth places respectively. A thunderstorm before the race, however, threw practice calculations aside: Fabi's team manager persuaded him to start on slicks like Cecotto, while Boutsen had to stay on wet-weather tyres as the different Bridgestone tyre sizes meant that the Spirit team needed practically an hour to change their car from wet to dry settings. To begin with, the Belgian made the most of the wet conditions, pulling away in the lead at the rate of two seconds a lap, while Fabi (never an enthusiast for wet-weather driving) tried hard down in eighth place just to keep his car on the road. Poor Cecotto was even worse off, having collided with a thoughtless Bellof on the opening lap and restarting three laps in arrears. But the track was drying rapidly, and Fabi was soon up to fifth, although 35 seconds behind his championship rival. Boutsen visited the pits for slicks just after quarter-distance, resuming in fourth place immediately ahead of the number one March: as Boutsen warmed his tyres, so Fabi nipped ahead. Approaching half-distance, the leading cars having also stopped for tyres, Fabi headed the race from a closing Boutsen. But a few laps later, Boutsen's tyres gave up the struggle and the Spirit

began dropping back, eventually to finish sixth, while Fabi stroked the March-BMW smoothly on to race and championship victory.

Emphasising that there was plenty of interest further down the field throughout the season, Beppe Gabbiani showed well whenever Maurer supplied him with equipment the equal of Bellof's; Philippe Streiff showed strongly in the AGS, finishing second at Vallelunga and Mantorp Park; Alessandro Nannini impressed in the Minardi despite mid-season problems with skirts and tyres, the Italian équipe ending up on M&H rubber; Mike Thackwell gave further proof of his outstanding ability on whichever tyres were going free at the meetings he attended; Frank Jelinski was a consistent finisher; Christian Danner showed considerable improvement since the previous year; Thierry Tassin shone at Silverstone, the Nürburgring and Spa before Docking-Spitzley ran out of equipment and money; and Jo Gartner proved fast in the poorly-prepared Merzario 822.

1983 – A Tale of Two Seasons

Spirit Racing's stay in the Formula was extremely brief, for during the winter they announced their intention to concentrate exclusively on a F1 project with Honda. The 201 chassis were sold to 'Pierre Chauvet', adapted to take Heidegger BMW units, and painted in Emco colours for 'Chauvet' and fellow-Austrian Jo Gartner to run on Bridgestone tyres.

Honda, however, remained a force in F2, continuing to supply their V6 engines (now claiming 340 bhp) to Ralt. The RH6 chassis would feature revised bodywork, a wider front track and pull-rod front suspension and would run on Michelin rubber. Drivers would be Jonathan Palmer and Mike Thackwell, Ron Tauranac considering these the best available.

March produced a totally new car in order to meet the survival cell safety regulations introduced for 1983. The 832, featuring honeycomb bulkheads, was narrower and tidier than its predecessor and also had strengthened suspension and a revised fuel system. Christian Danner was again responsible for the development of the car, and, because of March's growing Indycar commitments, the works effort would this year be entrusted to Mike Earle's Onyx Racing operation, who would run Beppe Gabbiani and Thierry Tassin alongside the German. The championship holders also helped establish the James Gresham Racing and Mint Engineering teams for drivers Enrique Mansilla, Dave Scott (both up from British F3) and Roberto del Castello, while Markus Hotz purchased a machine for Lamberto Leoni (returning to international motor racing following a serious illness) and San Remo Racing two cars for Paolo Barilla and Aldo Bertuzzi. The Gresham and Mint cars were contracted to Bridgestone, as opposed to the works' Michelins: Mint and San Remo would use Heidegger versions of the BMW motor, whilst Gresham would use Heine Mader units from the same manufacturer.

Heidegger power would also be employed by Maurer, the German team entering Stefan Bellof, and Alain Ferté in the F1-type (carbon-fibre construction and pull-rod front suspension) MM83s, while Paul Owens looked after the similar cars of Kenny Acheson and French F3 Champion Pierre Petit: the 'A' team would use Michelins, whilst Owens' 'B' team relied on Bridgestone rubber.

Philippe Streiff would campaign a singleton AGS this year, the tiny French team now without Motul sponsorship, but French interest in the Formula was heightened by the return of Martini, featuring a straightforward chassis powered by a Mader BMW, tyred by Michelin, sponsored by Marlboro and driven by Philippe Alliot, a graduate of the constructor's F3 équipe.

Minardi produced a stunning looking carbon-fibre and honeycomb chassis in the M283, albeit on contemporary F1 flat bottom lines (F1 cars had had to abandon skirts since 1982 for safety reasons, although the F2 constructors had successfully argued against such measures in their category until a further two years had elapsed). Drivers would be Alessandro Nannini and the unsponsored European F3 Champion Oscar 'Poppy' Larrauri. Another contender from Italy was the rather ugly Merzario for Guido Dacco and Fulvio Ballabio. The Minardis would use Michelin rubber while the Merzarios wore Japanese Dunlops. An attempt to keep the Formula's costs down this year by doing away with qualifying tyres was reflected in a new regulation under which 14 tyres for each car per meeting had to be designated prior to official practice.

The 12-race series featured the expected battle for honours between March-BMW and Ralt-Honda, albeit in a season curiously divided into two halves.

The first part of the season was dominated by the Roloil-liveried Onyx March of Beppe Gabbiani, taking over where Corrado Fabi had left off in 1982. In his fifth year of F2, the 25-year-old Italian showed a new-found maturity in his driving, powering the March to a convincing flag-to-flag victory at Silverstone, and following this success up with masterly defeats of Thackwell at Thruxton, Nannini at the Nürburgring (the chasing Minardi spinning away its chances of a win at the race's final corner) and Palmer at Vallelunga. Only at Hockenheim — dominated by Palmer's Ralt-Honda — did the combination fail to finish, and after five of the championship's 12 rounds Gabbiani enjoyed an impregnable-looking 14-point lead over Palmer, with Thackwell two points further down.

The half-way point, Pau, provided a farcical interlude which was also one of the best races of the year. The drivers lined up on the tricky street circuit in persistent drizzle, on the understanding the race would be stopped and restarted if the track became dry (the pits being inadequate to cope with wholesale tyre changes). After 20 of the 73 laps, the road surface was quite dry, Gabbiani leading from Thackwell (Ralt-Honda) and Alain Ferté (Maurer-BMW), but the signal to stop the proceedings never came and gradually cars began pulling into the pits to have slicks fitted. Gabbiani's driveshaft broke, while Thackwell was the victim of a chaotic pit-stop, and out of it all Jo Gartner (Spirit-BMW), still on the harder Bridgestone wets, hit the front from Palmer (Ralt-Honda), Acheson and Bellof (Maurers). After a few more laps, the rain came down again, catching out some of the contestants on slicks and causing further pit stops. Gartner and Acheson — still on their original wet-weather tyres — pulled further away in front, while down in seventh place Alain Ferté was the first competitor to persevere on slicks, despite over-shooting one corner and losing his Maurer's nosecone as a result. As the shower ended and the track dried once more, so Ferté began progressing up the field, his noseless car closing on the leaders at the rate of five seconds a lap. With just two laps to go, Ferté squeezed past Gartner to the crowd's delight to take the Maurer over the finish line first. Unfortunately, the young Frenchman's great drive ended in more farce when his car was disqualified for being underweight and victory was awarded to Gartner.

The second half of this schitzophrenic

Beppe Gabbiani made the most of his equipment in the first half of the season to take the March-BMW 832 to four race wins, including here at Thruxton.

The remainder of the year belonged to the Ralt-Honda team: the RH6H/83s of Mike Thackwell and Jonathan Palmer in 1–2 formation at Donington.

season belonged to the Ralt-Honda, and particularly to Dr Jonathan Palmer. The team had already built up an impressive reliability record, and further attention to the cars' weight and suspension transformed the Ralts' speed performance. Mike Thackwell did a 'Ferté' at Jarama, winning the race without his Ralt's nosecone, while Palmer came in third. At Donington, the team was in a class of its own all weekend: Palmer was over a second quicker than anyone else in practice and demoted his team mate after 18 laps to score Ralt-Honda's first 1-2 victory. Misano was an appallingly-run race meeting, featuring several major retirements, but again Jonathan finished first, while Enna saw him profit from Bellof's retirement and stave off a challenge from Streiff (the AGS now proving the fastest F2 car in a straight line) to get his hat-trick. Gabbiani finished fourth behind Thackwell, but, having failed to score in the previous four races, now trailed his English rival by 19 points.

All Palmer had to do to take the title was finish in the top three at the penultimate round at Zolder: while Gabbiani was knocked into retirement by Nannini as he swept up the field from a poor grid position, Palmer duly led from flag to flag with Thackwell behind for another 1-2. The last race, at Mugello, brought a similar result, except this time Thackwell mounted a stern challenge to his champion team mate and Palmer had to work hard to keep the New Zealander at bay over the last few laps, winning by 0.32 seconds. While the March runners scratched their heads over severe understeer problems, Palmer had chalked up his 11th consecutive finish of the season and his fifth win on the trot — a reliability record unequalled in the Formula at any time. Ralt-Honda fittingly became winners of the newly instituted F2 Constructor's Cup.

Unfortunately, the substantial costs of F2 racing had led to an unsettled season with several driver changes affecting interest in the championship. Lamberto Leoni moved to Gresham Racing after the opening round only to run out of funds by mid-season; Guido Dacco replaced Barilla at San Remo Racing and Fulvio Ballabio took his sponsorship to AGS, leaving Merzario to run Richard Dallest; Oscar Larrauri only managed four races with Minardi; Kenny Acheson stopped appearing in the Formula once he'd landed a Grand Prix seat with RAM Racing: Alain Ferté lost his Maurer drive after eight of the 12 championship rounds; and Thierry Tassin also ran out of funds, his Onyx March seat going to Dave Scott.

Amidst the usual runners, the Maurers had had a disappointing season (which included repossession of their Heidegger engines at the April Hockenheim meeting, the team using Mader motors thereafter), with Bellof and Alain Ferté showing strongly only on intermittent occasions; Philippe Streiff became a consistent front runner in the rapid AGS; Alessandro Nannini reverted to last year's Minardi in order to make his mark; Philippe Alliot did well to put the Martini on pole at Misano; Dave Scott headed the grid in his privateer March at Silverstone only to suffer appalling luck during the rest of the season until he joined the Onyx set-up; and World Sidecar Champion Rolf Biland impressed in Markus Hotz's March whenever his motorbike commitments allowed him to take part.

With the Ralt-Hondas dominating the latter half of the season in a way which had been predicted by the pundits for some time, there was inevitable talk at the end of the year that BMW would now turn their back on the Formula. However, the Bavarian company recognised that the Anglo-Japanese victory had been a closer-run thing than it first appeared on simple scrutiny of the results, and soon announced that their engines would continue in F2 after all, although no longer serviced direct from the factory due to the increasing demands of their successful F1 turbo project. With the equally competitive Hart engine waiting on the sidelines for use by the right kind of operation, and, as ever, a variety of car constructors and promising young drivers keen to take part in the category, F2 still looked to have a very healthy future ahead of it. However, this did not prevent the Formula One Constructors Association from muscling in during the winter of 1983 with ill-judged proposals for a new single-seater category employing the 3 litre normally-aspirated Ford engine, now that its Grand Prix days were over. FOCA's plans — aimed at establishing the new formula for the 1984 season — posed a severe threat to F2, as FOCA clearly wished to organise a new stepping-stone to F1 and there was simply not enough sponsorship monies around to finance both secondary formulas. With little interest being shown in the FOCA idea, FISA threw its support behind continuing F2, although a change in F2 regulations to a 3 litre capacity in the near future cannot be discounted.

2 Organisation

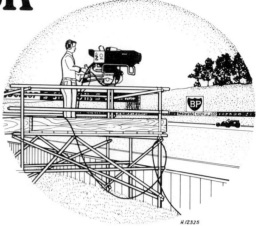

Like all other forms of motor sport, F2 is ultimately controlled by the Federation Internationale du Sport Automobile (FISA) which is the competition arm of the International Automobile Federation (FIA), which consists of motoring clubs from all over the world.

FISA creates international championships, carries out circuit safety inspections, registers speed records and each year publishes a calendar of approved international events. It is responsible for publishing and revising all rules governing the conduct of motor sport, including the various formula regulations, and ensures that these are enforced. The F2 text, for instance, contains regulations covering the cars' bodywork, weight, engines, transmissions, fuel, oil, water and electrical services, starting mechanisms, brakes, wheels, tyres, cockpits and a number of safety measures. In order to safeguard constructors' and other companies' investments, such rules can only be altered after two years' notice, with the exception of changes which are urgently required for safety reasons.

FISA's Executive Committee is assisted by a number of specialist commissions and working parties. The F2 Working Party comprises FISA's General Secretary, Yvon Léon, and technical adviser, Gabriel Cadringer, Emile Brézing (representing the race organisers' F2 Alliance) and Barry Bland (from the constructors' F2 Association). There are also regular, larger 'round table' meetings which focus particularly on technical progress and alterations to the Formula.

The F2 Association has played an important role in consolidating an harmonious, sporting atmosphere in F2 at a time when Grand Prix racing has become renowned for its cantankerous attitudes and continual sniping between FISA and the Formula One Constructors' Association (FOCA). In F2, the constructors first joined forces in the early 1970s, albeit in a pretty loose and ineffective fashion and with a fairly heady approach towards negotiations. In 1973, for instance, they threatened to stop building F2 cars altogether unless the sporting authorities and race organisers could guarantee increased race purses for the following season. The argument was won, but later the same year, the Association dissolved amidst various disagreements amongst the constructors themselves. By the end of 1975, however, the levels of prize money and travelling funds were once again a matter for concern, and so the F2 Association was revived by Hughes de Chaunac, at that time team manager with Alpine Elf.

The reformed association met at the circuits whenever problems arose or when changes affecting the Formula needed to be made. Barry Bland, of Motor Race Consultants — who had earlier negotiated a revised payments structure for F2 in which individual haggling over start money was replaced by a standard system of travel allowances and payments based on results — at that time represented the F2 privateer teams on the Association, but, in 1978, recognising that the Association needed to be established on a more professional basis, he offered to run the organisation from a central office with full-time staff. The Association is now constituted as a constructor-based body, although everyone competing in the Formula is kept abreast of developments. Policies are arrived at in consultation with customer teams and privateers, and technical and other issues agreed between the constructors and then proposed for adoption to FISA.

This approach of proceeding by means of consensus and 'gentlemen's agreements' has been extraordinarily successful. One of the

One of the F2 Association's tasks at race meetings is to help resolve any technical problems which might arise. Here, Christian Danner's March awaits entry to the scrutineering bay at Donnington.

Association's main concerns has been to keep the costs of competing in F2 as low as possible, and this aim has been pursued through a number of measures: agreeing not to carry out pre-race testing on circuits within a week of their hosting championship rounds; deciding not to use certain precious metals in racing car construction; and, more recently, proposing limiting the numbers of race tyres for use at each meeting. Since the Association's re-emergence, costs in F2 have risen less than the rate of inflation, and a season cost of £150,000 compares well with, say, a British F3 Championship season costing in the region of £100,000.

Technical issues have predictably proved the most problematic in resolving. An agreement not to use hydro-pneumatic suspensions, for instance, lasted for over a year until Maurer produced an adjustable, non-pneumatic suspension which they ran for most of 1982, causing Minardi to fit a pneumatic suspension system in protest. But here again, the teams' approach has been much more positive than in F1, for when agreements are broken it has been to pressure FISA into an early

clarification of the regulations, rather than to exploit any apparent loopholes.

Much of the Association's early work was concentrated on closing the traditional gap between entrants and race organisers. Meetings time-tables and the way races are run are agreed between the Association and the organisers, and the Association is represented at all race meetings to ensure that the team's needs are met, to liaise with the organisers and to act as an intermediary in any scrutineering problems which might arise. The Formula's financial structure has been revised once more, so that there is a fixed prize money scale, fixed travel allowances payable to the first 25 qualifiers and additional payments dependant on grid positions.

The F2 Association has also been very active in general promotion of the category. It is able to have some negotiation with organisers on race dates prior to FISA's official calendar being published, and prefers a list which does not place excessive demand on teams' organisational and travelling abilities and gives as much scope as possible (usually by avoiding Grand Prix week-

Television coverage is an important ingredient in the organisation of F2 race meetings.

ends) for television coverage – an all-important ingredient for sponsors. Most European Championship rounds now receive national television coverage, and the Association has involved itself in organising television showings elsewhere, as often countries wish to increase their coverage if one of their home drivers emerges as a strong championship contender. F2 race programmes have been sold to nations as diverse as Zimbabwe and Venezuela, and American and Mexican networks have transmitted regular showings of the races which make up the F2 season.

Hand in hand with this activity has been the Association's promotion of F2 outside Europe. Apart from the long-established Japanese Championship (boasting eight races in 1983), F2 cars also appear regularly in Formula Libre races throughout the world, and the Association has been involved in talks about pukka F2 races taking place in South Africa and in South America. In 1982, the Association and the F2 Alliance together proposed to FISA the establishment of a

F2 World Cup based on linked series of races in Europe, South America and Japan, and – although FISA's response was to apply all the thinking to a Formula Atlantic championship instead – the possibility still remains of worldwide F2 competition in the future.

Undoubtedly, the relatively low level of sponsorship involvement in F2 compared to F1, and the former's basis as a customer formula, has helped maintain a highly sporting ambience with no trace of the kind of acrimony which often bedevils Grand Prix racing. For the enthusiast, this has meant stable provision of a highly competitive single-seater formula in which the winner on the road is usually the real winner as well! This achievement has been a great credit to all those involved in F2 – organisers, competitors and constructors – who, although taking part in the Formula primarily for commercial reasons, nevertheless have always been aware that the combined outcome of their activities centres on a colourful and exciting show for spectators.

3 The Circuits

F2 racing takes place on many of Europe's most interesting circuits. Some of them (like Silverstone and Hockenheim) are tests of man and machine, others (like the Nürburgring and Pau) are legendary Grand Prix venues and still more (like Donington and Mugello) are gathering respected reputations. As with most racing calendars, the fixtures alter a bit from season to season — Brands Hatch is an infrequent venue, Spa ran F2 events until it regained its Grand Prix, Spain is showing increasing interest in F2 — but below is a selection of the racetracks which have featured most often in F2 over the years.

SILVERSTONE has become the traditional curtain-raiser of the F2 season. The cars speed round the 2.93 mile airfield circuit, but there's always an atmosphere of unpreparedness as drivers and teams get to grips with their new machines for the first time in race conditions. The Spring fixture is often affected by rain as well, which makes predicting a race winner even more difficult! The fastest circuit on the calendar, Silverstone is situated near Towcester, Northants.

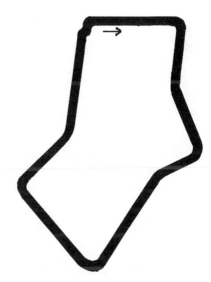

SILVERSTONE

Through the spray at Silverstone.

THRUXTON (near Andover, Hants) is another airfield circuit — the British Automobile Racing Club's successor to their Goodwood track. As well as being fast (the F2 lap record is currently 125.28 mph), this rather featureless 2.36 mile circuit has also become extremely bumpy, making racing a boring but dangerous affair for the drivers. The tight Campbell-Cobb-Segrave section and the Club chicane are the best spots for viewing, given that the circuit's most important corner — the flat-out right-hander at Church — is not accessible to spectators.

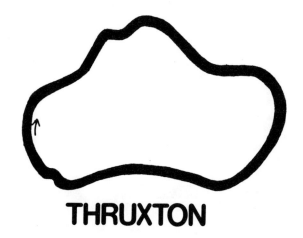

THRUXTON

Entering the chicane from the fast sweeps of Thruxton.

HOCKENHEIM seems like two different circuits. On the one hand, there's the long, rapid back loop through pine forest, where speeds have had to be kept down in recent years by the introduction of artificial chicanes, and on the other there's the twisting stadium section dwarfed by the massive grandstands which hold most of the track's spectators. F2 has always been a popular attraction at Hockenheim, one of the few places where drivers can actually hear the crowd urging them on above the noise of their engines. The Elf and Sachskurves are particularly good areas to watch from on the 4.22 mile course, near Heidelberg, West Germany.

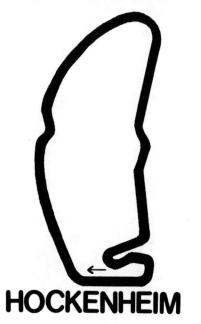

HOCKENHEIM

In the stadium section at Hockenheim.

THE NÜRBURGRING remained a regular venue for the F2 circus long after its rejection by the Grand Prix world in 1977. There's no doubt that the old 14.17 mile course, with its hundreds of twists and turns through the Eifel Mountains, was too lengthy to provide safety measures up to modern F1 standards, nevertheless it formed a unique measure of driving skills and was often the scene of phenomenal individual performances. From 1984, a newly-built 2.81 mile track will be used — without such features as the saucer-shaped Karussel and the Pflanzgarten hump where the cars were launched into the air, it is hard to envisage it attracting the classic status of its adjacent ancestor.

NÜRBURGRING

Approaching the Karussel on the Nürburgring.

MUGELLO, situated amidst the Tuscany Hills north of Florence, was originally the centre of a 41.1 mile road course which formed part of the famous Mille Miglia route. Now, it features a challenging 3.2 mile circuit nestling in a valley, with 16 various corners curving up and down both sides of the bowl. With first-class safety measures and a track wide enough to allow for numerous overtaking opportunities, Mugello provides excellent viewing for spectators, and many enthusiasts consider it to be amongst Europe's finest circuits.

MUGELLO

Winding up the hillside at Mugello.

VALLELUNGA, a purpose-built autodrome north of Rome, is luxurious by Italian standards, featuring permanent snack-bars and toilets as part of the large tribune grandstands which overlook the entire circuit apart from the rapid Curva dei Cimini. For the drivers, overtaking on the narrow track can pose a problem, but Vallelunga's tighter corners provide several outbraking possibilities, so the cars usually manage to get past each other one way or another!

VALLELUNGA

Startline view from Vallelunga's grandstands.

PAU — a town in the French Pyrenees — is the oldest venue on the F2 calendar, the present street circuit first being used in 1935, when Nuvolari won in an Alfa Romeo. Since 1964, the Grand Prix de Pau has been held for F2 cars rather than F1, the combination of up-and-coming drivers and a demanding but fast course providing some unique moments. Unlike Monaco, Pau has no smoothed kerbs or flattened gutters, while the full-throttle armco-lined Parc Beaumont curve is a real test of drivers' courage. Held over Pentecost weekend, the Pau meeting has an atmosphere all of its own, as the townspeople gather to see this season's young lions duelling over roads which they themselves are used to motoring along more sedately the rest of the year.

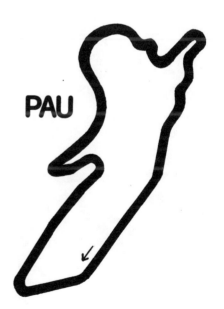

Picturesque Pau.

MISANO's Autodrome Santamonica consists of three flat, uninspiring loops which nevertheless provide for good and rapid racing, albeit on a narrow track with little opportunity for passing manoeuvres. A couple of miles inland from Rimini — the Italian equivalent of Blackpool — and the popular Adriatic coast, the 2.17 mile circuit is often bathed in oppressive heat for its F2 fixture. The venue has long been renowned for its autocratic officials and in 1983 the whole Maurer team withdrew following Stefan Bellof's disqualification at the end of practice for allegedly threatening to hit the Clerk of the Course!

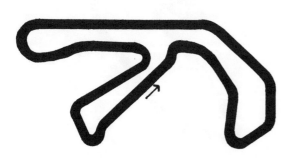

Leaving Misano's pits and startline area.

MISANO

ENNA's heyday occurred during the 1960s, when the ultra-fast Sicilian circuit was first opened. The 2.98 mile track circling Lake Pergusa witnessed many heady slipstreamer races which called more upon drivers' courage and stamina than any of their driving skills. On several occasions, the racing was further enlivened by the need to pull errant competitors from the snake-infested marshes lining the course! With the advent of downforce and increasing speeds and turbulence, it all became too dangerous, though, and from 1970 chicanes were introduced to slow things down. Since then, kerb-hopping has become part and parcel of Enna events, although by 1983 the kerbs were high enough to demand some precision from the F2 drivers after all.

Round the lake at Enna.

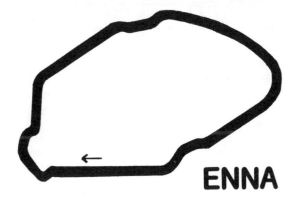

DONINGTON PARK (near Castle Donington, Leicestershire) was the scene of unforgettable tussles between the mighty German Mercedes and Auto Union teams in 1937 and '38, but was requisitioned for military use on the outbreak of the Second World War. Although the track was ruined by the time the land was returned to its owners, local businessman and racing enthusiast Tom Wheatcroft dreamt of bringing motor sport back to Donington. He finally bought the venue himself, and in 1977 saw a new 1.96 circuit brought into use. A fast and tricky course, constructed within the outline of its predecessor and offering superb viewing, Donington has acquired an enviable reputation, while the Donington Collection racing car museum houses the world's largest display of Grand Prix machines.

Through Donington's curves.

4 Getting Started

For most drivers (and some teams), F2 is an important rung in the ladder which leads up to F1.

Most F2 competitors will have already been involved in racing single-seater cars for a number of years. Their careers almost invariably began in low-cost national single-seater formulas like Formule Renault (France), the Fiat based Formula Italia, Volkswagen-derived SuperVee (Germany) or Formula Ford (Germany and Britain) — often following completion of race driving courses at schools like the Winfield School at Magny Cours or Motor Racing Stables at Brands Hatch.

Of these categories, Formula Ford is the most widely-found, having been inaugurated in 1967 with race driving schools in mind. The initial 1600cc Formula proved so popular that in 1974 an additional 2000cc category was introduced. In both cases, the cars are spaceframe chassis using specified engines and standard tyres: FF2000 cars also have rear wings which enable their drivers to get to grips with the importance of racing car aerodynamics and balance.

A new FF1600 car will cost approximately £6,000, with a further £1,500 required for the engine, although it is quite possible to make your mark among the host of Formula Ford championships with a secondhand car costing considerably less. At this stage in their careers, some drivers will prepare their cars themselves, while others hire mechanics or use preparation teams who will loan race-prepared machinery and offer a day's advance testing at the circuit at a cost of £800–£1,000 per race meeting. This formula caters for all kinds of budgets — on the one hand, it's possible to approach it on a race-by-race basis which could cost as little as £450 a time, on the other a year with a works Formula Ford team will set you back some £30,000!

Several drivers' first experience of continental motor racing takes the form of qualifying rounds for the European FF2000 Championship, held on a variety of interesting circuits and often as supporting races at Grand Prix meetings.

Others prefer to remain home-based for another year or two and progress instead to participate in their national F3 championships.

F3 is universally regarded as the first professional single-seater category and races take place all over Europe, the most prestigious national series being held in Britain, France and Italy. The cars are powered by 2000cc production-based engines, incorporate 'ground effect' technology and require even more know-how from their pilots in terms of settings and driving than does Formula Ford. In Britain, one type of tyre is stipulated, although elsewhere in Europe there is a free choice of rubber. The races remain virtual sprints — each practice session and the race itself are unlikely to last more than 20 minutes — although the championship series can be lengthy. The 1983 Marlboro British F3 Championship, for instance, took place over 20 events between March and October and required a budget of approximately £100,000 to mount a competitive effort.

Some F3 races are regarded as more important than others — for example, the supporting events to the British and Monaco Grands Prix have long received huge entries and attract substantial interest from F1 team managers and media alike. Whilst some drivers do manage to make the massive leap from F3 to F1, at the end of the national F3 season most of the successful runners contemplate entering either the European F3 or F2 series for the coming year.

The European F3 Championship has gained in stature in recent years, although it costs nearly as much as a F2 season and offers little progress

Stefan Bellof was twice winner of the German Formula Ford Championship before graduating into F2.

Argentinian Enrique Mansilla was one driver to move into F2 after competing in the British F3 Championship.

79

80 *1980 European F3 Champion Michele Alboreto at the prestigious supporting event to the Monaco Grand Prix.*

to the top national F3 drivers. F2, on the other hand, is a more professional category, involving bigger cars and more powerful engines, a greater level of competitiveness throughout the field and hour-long practice sessions and races in which drivers can build up their stamina and develop a sense of race strategy.

In the past three seasons, an average of 32% of regular F2 contenders have arrived in the Formula from F3, 9% as European F3 graduates and the other 21% from the F3 championships of Britain, Italy, France and Germany. Of these, though, it is the former European F3 runners who are most likely to start F2 with a works drive — a reflection of the variety of European constructors involved in F2. Most of the remainder of the ex-F3 racers take part in their first F2 season driving for customer teams.

Geoff Lees had an unhappy time with the F1 Shadow team before returning to F2 in 1981.

Christian Danner's drives in a BMW M1 persuaded the Bavarian firm to introduce him to single-seater racing via F2.

World Sidecar Champion Rolf Biland is the latest in a line of successful motorcyclists to forge a four-wheeled career in F2.

But most drivers will remain in F2 for more than one season. No one has won the European Championship in their first season of F2 racing since Mike Hailwood in 1972, and so many of the privateer newcomers to the Formula will be hoping their initial year's performance will be good enough to persuade sponsors and team officials to place them in works cars for the following year. Over the past three seasons, an average of 47% of regular F2 contestants had raced in the category before.

This figure has been growing in recent years and reflects the mounting difficulties of gaining entry to an increasingly expensive F1, many drivers preferring to remain in F2 (and diversify their driving activities in saloon and sportscar racing) than raise a huge budget in order to enter Grand Prix racing driving for a no-hope team. Other drivers who have taken the Grand Prix path — like Geoff Lees and Beppe Gabbiani — will sometimes now return to F2 in order to re-establish their case for a decent F1 opportunity.

As with all professional motor racing categories, sponsorship plays a large part in securing seats in F2, and the right backing will obtain F2 drives for people with previous racing experience which has not involved single-seaters. Christian Danner, for instance, was picked up by BMW after he had competed in Germany's G5 saloon series, while Johnny Cecotto and Rolf Biland were able, as world motorcycle champions, to attract sufficient backing to begin their four-wheeled racing careers in the Formula.

It is the momentum of sponsorship which can sometimes cause a F3 driver to miss F2 and jump straight into F1. Because of the huge differences between the two formulas in terms of power and race length, however, there is a growing body of opinion within the sport which feels that such progression is downright dangerous and that F2 should become a mandatory link between the two categories. F3 drivers have simply not developed the stamina necessary to compete in lengthy Grands Prix, and F2 provides an ideal training ground for such events. At present, a different driving technique is required, as F2 continues to employ the ground effect approach which F1 has been forced to jettison on safety grounds, but from 1985 this disparity will disappear and F2 cars will be as flat-bottomed as their F1 counterparts.

5 Sponsorship

Although its costs have risen by less than the rate of inflation in recent years, F2 is by no means the inexpensive racing category it once was. It involves highly sophisticated machinery, and the competition is such that a heavy premium is placed on mid-season testing for racing-car and tyre development. Running a car in the seven-month, 12-race European Championship therefore costs in the region of £140–190,000.

In most instances, it is the drivers who must raise such sums of money in order to take part in the sport. Although sometimes the teams will take it upon themselves to attract funding (for instance, Spirit's package proposal to Marlboro for the 1982 season), it is nowadays very rare for a driver not to pay for a seat in F2. In 1983, for example, only Ralt — backed by Honda and the Casio sponsorship which the Japanese car company had brought to the team — were known to be in a position to be able to pay their drivers, although it was rumoured that Stefan Bellof was not paying for his position as number one Maurer driver, and the Italian Minardi concern was prepared to run European F3 Champion Oscar Larrauri for next to nothing.

As things turned out, Larrauri lost his drive before mid-season, while a number of other young hopefuls — among them Thierry Tassin, Frank Jelinski, Lamberto Leoni, Alain Ferté and Enrique Mansilla — were unable to enter all the championship rounds due to difficulties with their budgets. Teams will not agree a contract with a driver until he can guarantee most of the season's sponsorship income, although the money itself is often delivered in phased payments over the course of the year. In F2, even the works cars are often run by a separate operation from the constructing company, and so most teams need to cover the cost of their initial investment in purchasing cars and machinery as soon as possible.

A F2 season undoubtedly represents excellent value for drivers and sponsors alike. A year in British F3 now costs around £100,000, while European F3 requires almost the same outlay as F2, but neither of the F3 series enjoys the television and press coverage afforded to F2. The costs involved in taking part in F1 are, of course, astronomical, but the successful F2 driver will be better prepared for Grand Prix competition than someone straight out of F3, and is likely to be required to pay less for a F1 drive than someone who is relatively inexperienced.

For most drivers, the hunt for sponsorship forms a continual undercurrent to their racing activities. Some of the best driver-sponsor relationships are forged early on in a driver's career and are developed as the driver progresses through the various formulas. Examples of such link-ups have been Swedish cough-drop manufacturer SMOG'S support for Ronnie Peterson, Marlboro backing for Stefan Johansson and Thierry Boutsen and the Guiness brewery's association with Derek Daly.

Current British F1 racer Derek Warwick entered F2 in 1979 in a BP Oil-sponsored semi-works March after winning BP's F3 Championship the previous season. BP were keen to promote their light viscosity oil, VF7, and organised a highly effective campaign around their championing of a talented young British driver in the cut-and-thrust of European F2. On the track, the season wasn't a great success, but both driver and sponsors had realistically regarded it as a learning period, and the following year, BP — keen to back an effort capable of winning the European Championship itself — decided to support the two-car Toleman team, running Warwick and another BP-backed driver, Stephen South, in a practically all-British effort (ironically receiving most of its financial assistance from Italian tyre manufacturers Pirelli, who were using F2 as a testing ground for their product's eventual use in F1). Pre-season events saw South replaced by Brian Henton, who went on to win the championship, with Warwick as runner-up. BP again ran a very visual campaign, backing up their on-track successes with media adverts, in-store promotions and links with corporate promotions like the 'Challenge to Youth' scheme. BP's research division took the opportunity to liaise with Toleman's engine supplier, Brian Hart, to their mutual benefit, and, at the season's end, all parties were happy to venture together into F1, where BP retained an involvement with Toleman and Warwick for three more years.

Most drivers who have established such long-term sponsorship links still need to raise further backing from other sources as their rise through the formulas subjects them to increasing expense. Sponsorship demands almost as much concentration as the racing itself. Throughout each season, the drivers make as many introductions as possible with potential sponsors, and over the winter they contact companies in the hope of attracting money for the forthcoming year, sometimes with assistance from the teams who require their services and have made their own contacts during several years of F2 competition, or from professional driver promotion agencies. With the help of March, for instance, Dave Scott in 1982 wrote to 400 mainly British companies in search of backing — and without success!

Sponsorship response will, of course, depend to some extent on the general economic situation and on the national awareness and reaction to motor sport, and to F2 racing in particular. With the occasional exception — such as BP's and ICI's involvement a few years ago and the Matchbox toy firm's support of Surtees in the early seventies — British industry has proved notoriously unresponsive to sponsorship approaches for F2 participants. Despite the category's increasing popularity and growing television coverage, most British companies seem sadly reluctant to promote themselves to the extent called for by F2 race budgets. It's interesting to note that in Italy, which has a similarly poor economy, but where motor racing is adored, there appears to be relatively little difficulty in drumming up such finance, as witness the large numbers of Italian sponsors, teams and drivers engaged in both F1 and F2; obviously, the

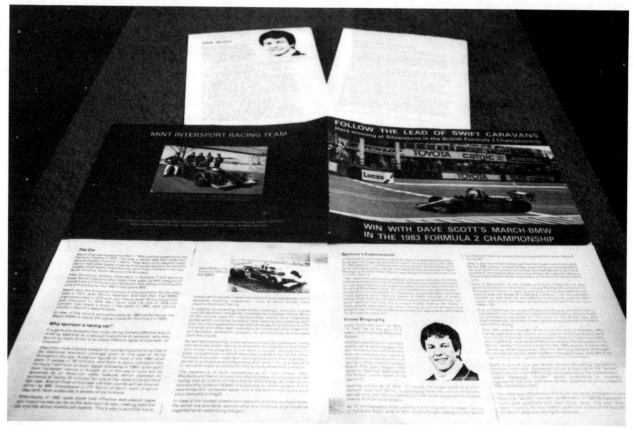

Dave Scott's sponsorship-seeking literature circulated prior to his 1983 F2 season.

Derek Warwick and his BP-backed March pose beside a BP Lubricants tanker at the oil company's Fulham terminal.

ways in which motor sport is promoted can have an important bearing on the availability of sponsorship.

The most imaginative commercial use of F2 — and an example to the industrial might of other countries — can be credited to the French petrol company Elf, who were involved in the category for ten years from 1967. Their activities not only placed a new trade-name firmly in the public consciousness, but also played a central role in restoring French motor racing fortunes.

Elf was formed by the French Government in 1967, following the discovery of oil in the French Sahara, to provide France with oil and gas. Its management decided the young company should establish a go-getting, innovatory image and immediately associate with three 'vanguard' projects — the French Aerotrain, Concorde and motor racing with Matra, the French missile manufacturers who had been constructing racing cars for the previous two years.

Elf's interest in motor racing would be no overnight affair, for the company was determined to effect a long-term policy aimed at assisting French racing-car constructors, drivers and team managers, broadening motor sport's media attention and collecting technical data arising from competition for application in future development of lubricants and fuels. A four-year contract was signed with Matra, with the aim of winning the French F3 Championship in 1967, the European

F2 Championship in 1968, the F1 World Championship in 1969 and Le Mans in 1970 (remarkably, three of these four ambitious targets were met, Elf having to wait until 1978 before they won Le Mans with Renault).

After 1979, Matra chose to restrict their activities to F1 and sportscar racing and formed a racing partnership with Simca, whose oil supplier was Shell. Elf began to broaden their links with Renault (similarly state-backed) and remained committed to F2 as the best testing ground for the new wave of French talent (now coming up through the ranks of the Elf-assisted Formule France) against international oppositon. After backing the poorly-prepared French constructors Pygmée in 1970, Elf restricted their support to French drivers in 1971, financing Cevert, Depailler and Jabouille in Italian Tecnos. The following year saw the introduction of the Alpine-designed Elf 2, albeit under English management, Elf deciding to maximise their public exposure and establish a test-bed set-up which might eventually lead to a Grand Prix Elf 1. By 1974, the cars were in the hands of two all-French teams and driven by former Elf-Alpine F3 racers and Patrick Tambay, fresh out of the Elf-backed Formule Renault. In the wake of Cevert's death at Watkins Glen, Elf also decided to sponsor the works March-BMW of France's next most promising hope, Patrick Depailler, who won the European Championship.

The following year saw a further expansion in

Companies advertise their F2 involvement throughout Europe.

A sponsor's dream photo? – Patrick Tambay steers the Elf 2 through Hockenheim's Elf Kurve.

Another car to adopt its sponsor's name in F2 was the Texaco Star, née Lotus 74, which, despite the driving talents of Emerson Fittipaldi and Ronnie Peterson, proved singularly unsuccessful.

Elf's F2 activities, the company sponsoring European Champion Jacques Laffite in a Martini-BMW, while their other four drivers took the runner-up positions. The category had now become a French-dominated formula except in terms of engine-power. But Elf had already successfully pressed for a change in regulations from 1976 and had provided Renault with £40,000 to develop the 1.5-litre Gordini V6, which reigned supreme in F2 for the next two years, the Jean Sage-managed Elf stable winning the championship with Jabouille in 1976 and René Arnoux taking Martini to their second title in 1977.

By now, Elf felt ready to take on the Grand Prix establishment with the ambitious Renault project, running a turbo-charged version of the F2 V6, and with Ligier; the company ceased its direct involvement with F2, although since then it has used its motor sport contacts to further the careers of other Elf Formule Renault and F3 drivers, such as Alain Prost, Richard Dallest, Philippe Streiff and Alain Ferté.

Throughout Elf's association with F2, the company profited from extensive advertising in France of its sporting activities and also produced F2 racing films for television stations around the world.

As well as sponsoring teams and drivers, the French petrol company also lent their name to F2 race meetings. By 1983, race organisers were required to pay out £37,500 per round to F2 competitors, as well as the promotional and organisational costs involved in running an international race meeting. On top of spectator gate receipts, organisers are keen to acquire race sponsorship and income from television coverage. Nowadays, several events are sponsored by Marlboro, the multinational tobacco company providing budgets nationally for races and drivers.

Although F2 is recognised by sponsors as a crucial step in the evolution of motor racing careers, and a sport which attracts substantial attention, it has fortunately avoided becoming dominated by commercial considerations. For the enthusiast, this has meant that F2 has gained in stature and professionalism over the years, but with a continuing desire for close competition, featuring drivers who have reached the Formula more because of their talents behind the wheel than their wealth.

F2 race sponsorship provides another opportunity for publicity.

6 Formula 2 Cars

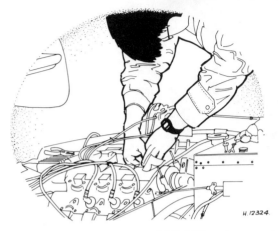

H.12324.

With F2 chassis costing £30,000 apiece and each engine over £12,000, it's not surprising that the Formula involves highly technical and race-tuned machinery.

In effect, the Formula requires scaled-down Grand Prix cars. The regulations state that the machines must be single-seaters employing no more than four wheels, while unsuper-charged engines of up to 2000cc are permitted provided they have no more than six cylinders. The cars must be driven by two wheels only, and there is a limit of five gearbox ratios (excluding reverse). The overall width of the vehicles — including the open wheels — must not exceed 200cm and no parts can be higher than 90cm above ground level other than safety roll-over bars. Minimum weight is set at 515 kilograms.

Unlike F1 cars, which now have mandatory flat bottoms, F2 chassis and bodywork are still built to ground effect criteria. Sliding skirts are banned, and the teams have agreed not to introduce hydro-pneumatic suspension systems: the regulations assert that no part of the bodywork or of the suspended part of the car can be lower than 4cm above the ground, but the succeeding rule which forbids any device "intended to change the ground clearance of the bodywork or of the entirely sprung part of the car, whether partially and/or temporarily" has caused a good deal of controversy and disquiet. At the begining of 1983, FISA announced they would be using laser beams to test that the bodywork on F2 runners remained 4cm from the road at speed, but in the event this never produced clear readings and checks were carried out through the use of 'hockey sticks' at the end of the pit-lane — which meant that bodywork could still be lowered to ground level at speed and a team not be penalised. Fortunately,

from 1985, F2 cars will be flat-bottomed in line with their F1 counterparts, and the problem eliminated.

FISA also prescribes a number of safety measures. Fuel tanks must be FIA-approved rubber bladders and, like oil tanks, are housed within a sandwich-construction crushable structure designed to minimise the risk of fire in the event of accident impact. The cars also carry two fire extinguishers — one in the cockpit and the other in the engine compartment — and a spark-proof electrical circuit-breaker capable of being triggered both internally by the driver and externally. The brake system must have two separate circuits operated by the same pedal, so that, should one circuit fail for any reason, the brake pedal will still operate the brakes on at least two wheels. The driver himself sits in a strengthened 'survival cell': he wears two shoulder strap safety belts, one abdominal strap and two crotch straps, and a flame-resistant pipe leads from his helmet to a medical air bottle fitted into his car. Finally, all cars must contain two roll-over structures designed to protect the driver in the event of their over-turning, and must also carry a red warning light at the rear.

Chassis

The formula is currently contested by eight makes of chassis — March, Ralt, Maurer, AGS, Minardi, Martini, Spirit and Merzario (old Lola-built Tolemans appeared on occasions in 1983, but only whilst San Remo Racing awaited their new March 832s). Of these, March and Maurer supply to customer operations as well as to their own racing teams; the Spirit presence involved an ambitious privateer set-up which purchased the Honda-engined chassis from the factory and

A selection of Maurer bodywork adorns the pits.

The 'hockey-stick' test applied to Palmer's Ralt-Honda.

converted them to run with BMW power; and the rest confine their activities to works efforts.

For several years now, March has been the most common chassis in use in F2. Although the cars' BMW engines are outpowered by the Honda V6 it is difficult for Honda users to run on the weight limit without spending a large amount of money, and so March have pinned their hopes on a light but sturdy chassis which is easy to maintain from the customer's point of view and not too difficult to set up for the different circuits. Their narrow 832 monocoque featured honeycomb bulkheads, while the engine was held in place by two very light horizontally-placed honeycomb arms rather than the normal tubular frame. A one-piece underbody produced a clean flow of air all the way back to the rear wheels, while the conventional top rocker/bottom wishbone suspension arrangement was designed so as to maximise the car's aerodynamics. For 1984,

Front end of the March-BMW 832, showing pedal box, brake fluid reservoirs and mandatory fire extinguisher.

March-BMW 832 cockpit.

March will employ pull-rod front suspension, while the engine will be placed at a four degree tilt to increase venturi size at the rear end of the machine.

Although they also supply their cars to privateer teams (at the same price as March), Maurer have set the standard in neat, expensive-looking and well-engineered F2 chassis incorporating many F1 design features. Their monocoque is made of carbon-fibre and honeycomb for lightness, and the car's narrowness is assisted by Maurer's own gearbox design, which incorporates the oil tank and an over-the-top change system compared to Hewland's side-change mechanism. The exhaust system fits under the bodywork, separated by a layer of heat-resistant material, while fashionable pull-rod suspension is employed at the front end. Maurer use a spring system (as have Ralt and AGS) which has an effect of lowering the chassis and bodywork at speed, although it also makes the cars more difficult to set up.

Minardi have also adopted a high-technology approach, producing a striking carbon-fibre and honeycomb chassis for 1983 with pull-rod suspension and fully enclosed bodywork. Unfortunately, the design was based more on F1 flat bottom thinking than F2's ground effect situation; the car handled badly, and the Italian team had to revert to their more conventional-looking 1982 chassis for any chance of good results.

From being a production car constructor, Ralt for the past two years have imposed no production restrictions on their F2 chassis, aiming to produce out-and-out race winners instead. Their car is designed around the ground-effect venturi tunnels — the monocoque being just wide enough to accomodate the driver! — and the Honda V6 installation, the stressed-member engine requiring a larger fuel capacity than the BMW unit. The rear suspension incorporates an

Ready to go. . . Beppe Gabbiani's helmet is attached to a medical air bottle at the rear of the March cockpit.

The emphasis at March is on a sturdy but lightweight chassis straightforward to work on and simple to set up.

One of the many 1983 privateer Marches, this one driven by Japanese Kasuyoshi Hoshino àt Donington.

Bertram Schäfer's Maurer-BMW MM82 driven by Frank Jelinski at Thruxton.

inboard spring/damper system thanks to a modification of the Hewland FT200 gearbox, while the magnesium uprights are kept in the airstream so as to cool the wheel bearings. Pull-rod suspension is now used at the front of the car, while flat top bodywork around the engine improves airflow to the injection trumpets and the rear wing.

AGS ended the 1983 season generally acknowledged as the fastest F2 machinery in a straight line. The tiny French firm's cars — produced on an extremely small budget — have benefited greatly from downforce evaluations at Michelin's Clermont Ferrand test track, these leading to a redesign of the side pods, with the single piece underbody enabling a clean airflow to the exit at the rear. The car's aerodynamics are also enhanced by adoption of pull-rod front suspension and horizontally-mounted rear dampers and twin springs at the top of the gearbox.

Fellow French constructors Martini returned to the Formula with a downward-tapering

Maurer-BMW MM83 (Stefan Bellof).

The striking Minardi M283 chassis.

Ventilated front brake disc (Ralt-Honda).

aluminium sheet monocoque with honeycomb underbody. Suspension was initially conventional rocker and wishbone all round, although a second chassis was produced during the season with the pull-rod system at the front. The BMW engine is held in place by a steel frame.

The Spirit chassis, run by the Austrian Emco Sports team, was neatly adapted to accept the BMW unit as a non-stressed member (unlike its Japanese predecessor). The monocoque is all-aluminium honeycomb, with high tapering sides — originally constructed with the car's large fuel capacity in mind — affording driver protection, and features inboard spring/damper units at both front and rear. The fabricated front and rear uprights incorporate cooling systems designed to keep bearings and brakes at optimum working temperatures.

The most ungainly-looking and poorly engineered car in F2 is undoubtedly the Italian Merzario. A monocoque with carbon-fibre elements and pull-rod suspension, its only competitive showing in the wet at Pau was due more to the skills of driver Richard Dallest than anything else.

Engines

The 1983 season saw a continuation of the battle between the Honda V6 and the four-cylinder BMW engines. The Japanese racing unit claims 340bhp at 10,700rpm and consists of a cast-iron block, aluminium head and magnesium camcover. Rebuilds are carried out by the Japanese en-

gineers seconded to Ralt or at John Judd's Engine Developments, where the high-revving Honda B67 was improved with revised heads in 1981. A noisy motor, giving good power out of corners, the purpose-built Honda enjoys twice as much useful mileage between rebuilds as its BMW rival.

The BMW M12 has long been available from a variety of sources. The factory engines (supplied exclusively to the works March team for the past ten years) were built by Paul Rosche of BMW Motorsport Gbmh, who originally designed the four-cylinder unit as a 1600cc road car engine in the 1950s. Despite opposition from pure racing engines like Renault and Honda, Rosche somehow managed to extract enough extra power from it each year for the motor to remain competitive, and, although arguably the least powerful of the BMW variants on offer, the unit was highly reliable. BMW's growing F1 programme, however, caused the company to cease its direct involvement in F2 at the end of 1983, although the M12 will continue to be made available through Swiss engineer Heine Mader.

Mader's preparation firm has in the past taken on a lot of the work which the BMW factory organisation was too small to cope with, for, although based in Switzerland, Mader has worked very closely with Rosche. Mader F2 customers receive what are basically Rosche specification engines, with a few conservative detail alterations added for good measure. A less powerful, long distance engine is also available for those privateers, operating on a shoestring, who are less able to meet the costs of the frequent rebuilds needed by the top-notch M12.

A Lichtenstein engineer who used to work

Ralt-Honda RH6H/83 (Jonathan Palmer).

with Rosche, Max Heidegger, has a reputation as the most radical of the BMW engine specialists. His units feature a different internal oil system and a short stroke and are phenomenally powerful — but they will last only 150 miles (compared to Rosche's 250) and can be very unreliable.

The Mader and Heidegger BMWs are usually acquired through leasing deals, a team paying a standard rebuild fee plus, say, £2,000 per race for use of a freshly rebuilt engine and retention of the engine used at the previous meeting.

Currently on the sidelines of F2 is the light alloy-block Hart 420R engine, derived from the Ford Escort BDA powerplant by former F2 racer Brian Hart, and winner of the 1980 European Championship in the back of the Tolemans. This four-cylinder engine is highly reliable and is generally reckoned to be competitive with the Honda V6, the British unit enjoying a substantial weight advantage. Indeed, the weight differential is such that installation of a Hart in a March chassis entails considerable weight redistribution, which few runners are prepared to undertake. The only serious Hart-powered foray in 1983 was a one-off appearance by ex-F1 driver Derek Daly at Donington, where lack of grip and a fuel pick-up problem prevented his March 822 from making a good showing.

The Ferrari V6 was last seen in 1982 in the back of a Minardi chassis, but may make a comeback in the future. A heavy engine with a low sump which causes substantial installation problems, its one and only F2 success came at Misano in 1977. By the end of 1983, there were two other V6 engine possibilities in the pipeline — a blanked-off, 2-litre conversion of the now-obsolete F1 Cosworth DFV V8 unit, and a two-stroke Folthera motor from Rolf Biland's motor-bike sidecar engine builder. Development of these designs, however, will depend on how long the Formula remains a 2-litre category.

Tyres

From 1973 to 1979, F2 was a one-make monopoly as far as tyres were concerned, but with Goodyear's withdrawal at the end of that period and the inability of their successors, Pirelli, to corner the category's commercial market, F2 has since become a very competitive field for tyre manufacturers.

Bridgestone — Japan's leading tyre company

AGS-BMW JH19 (Philippe Streiff).

The aluminium Martini 001 monocoque.

Although not built from Lego, the Emco Spirit-BMW was nevertheless a neat modification of the 1982 Honda-powered chassis!

— entered European F2 racing in 1981 (encouraged by Honda). At the time, many Pirelli customers were voicing their dissatisfaction with the Italian company's products, and the Japanese rubber soon proved extremely popular, being quick and forgiving: by the end of the season, Bridgestone had won the European Championship with Ralt and attracted a substantial customer market. Their main problem has been operating

12000 miles from their headquarters, and a permanent European base was established in 1983. On Michelin's entry to the Formula, Bridgestone's success diminished, their approach not helped by their unsystematic provision of tyre variations and by their decision last season to service three different types of chassis.

Michelin were persuaded into F2 in 1982 by BMW's marketing division and have since proved

Merzario-BMW M28 (Richard Dallest).

Japanese attention to the Honda V6 unit.

the tyre to beat, the French operation having the advantage of a European base, a highly consistent product and previous knowledge (either through F3 or F1) of the circuits visited by the F2 circus. Both their qualifying and race radials have the edge over rival firms' products, although Bridgestone have enjoyed a slight advantage in terms of wet race rubberwear.

Tyre contracts form a crucial element of a F2 season, and enable teams to carry out all-important mid-season development tests at reduced cost, and with both Bridgestone and Michelin supplying their tyres free of charge to selected runners (although the French company has announced that its tyres are to be offered on sale to all comers from 1984), it has been difficult for commercial operations like M&H and Avon to establish a competitive foothold in the Formula. Nevertheless, F2 is Avon's top single-seater platform, and the British firm is now dominant in

Straight out of the box — BMW personnel prepare a Rosche M12 engine.

A Heidegger BMW unit installed in one of the works Maurers.

The Hart 420R engine.

Treaded and slick Bridgestones.

the small customer market, although on odd occasions (usually via Swiss agent Markus Hotz) Japanese-manufactured Dunlops still find their way onto the European F2 scene.

Racewear

As F2 is one of the fastest, and therefore most dangerous, of motorsports, FISA insist that F2 drivers are properly clothed and equipped, particularly to guard against the likelihood of fire. The F2 driver wears layers of Nomex fire-resistant clothing from head to toe, including underwear, socks, balaclavas and race overalls (triple and quadruple layers can give between 25 and 48 seconds' extra protection in the event of a fiery accident). Crash helmets must be strong, but light enough to cope with the enhanced G-forces of ground effect: they should also be flame-resistant and fitted with splinter-proof visors and connections for the safety air line and for the intercom

March 832 designer Ralph Bellamy and Christian Danner linked up by intercom.

Avon Tyres on hand in the paddock.

system through which the driver communicates to the team manager or engineer during busy practice periods or at pit stops. Driving boots and gloves are also made from Nomex, but feature soft leather on the soles and underside of the hands so as to maximise feel of the steering wheel, hand controls and foot pedals.

H.12326

7 A Race Weekend

Twenty-four potent F2 cars pound round a cold, misty and spectatorless Donington race track. It's Thursday — just two days before the circuit hosts the eighth round of the 1983 European Championship — and amongst the chain of cars hurtling through Donington's bends is the Onyx works March-BMW No.3 driven by 21-year-old Englishman Dave Scott.

Dave had begun the F2 series in his own privately-run car after a written approach for sponsorship to over 400 mainly British companies at the end of 1982 had failed to raise the kind of money he needed to purchase a works drive. Fortunately, he was better placed than most British drivers facing a largely self-financed season. Ever since leaving school, Dave's main aim had been to become a professional racing driver, and his father had been keen to help him realise this ambition. Recognising that a serious approach to the sport would preclude full-time business involvement and that the family's existing baking company could not (for legal and tax reasons) sponsor Dave's racing efforts, father and son had jointly formed a new company, Mint Engineering, both to produce packaging for the bakery's products and to cover Dave's motor sport activities; Dave found himself in a position to contribute substantially towards his motor racing as well as having a business to fall back on should his driving career fail to develop.

The Scotts' partnership in British F3 with the Intersport Racing preparation set-up of Glen Waters (ex-chief mechanic to Mario Andretti at Team Lotus) had convinced them that they were capable of mounting their own competitive F2 effort. They decided to run a March chassis because of the Bicester company's excellent F2 record, its good spares service and well-run customer division. A tyre contract — a prerequisite

for inexpensive testing opportunities during the course of the season — was obtained with the Japanese Bridgestone company, and a leasing arrangement made with Lichtenstein engineer Max Heidegger, whose BMW engines were renowned for their sheer power.

Once March's Peter Mackintosh had suggested that Intersport become a two-car team by

Dave Scott.

Highspot of the season — fastest practice lap at Silverstone...

... and the lowpoint: with del Castello out on the warm-up lap, Dave's March is pushed off the track after failing to start at Vallelunga.

running Italian customer Roberto del Castello as well, the means of competing in all the championship races seemed assured. Dave continued to enjoy backing from Swift Caravans (supporters since his schoolboy karting days and providers of the caravan Dave sleeps in at the circuit over race weekends), and, soon after the season began, was able to secure additional sponsorship from Chesham BMW dealers Colver and Hencher.

Things had got off promisingly, with Dave securing fastest practice lap in the March at Silverstone to start the opening championship round from pole position, but thereafter very little had gone right for the Intersport team. Dave stalled his car on the Silverstone grid and recovered to no higher than ninth when the Heidegger blew at two-thirds distance. At Thruxton, Dave's inexperience showed when, running eleventh, he understeered off the course in another car's turbulence and damaged the suspension. Intersport's first continental sortie to Hockenheim ended with the March's crownwheel breaking on the warm-up lap, while at the next round at Nürburgring Dave could only finish in 11th place following tyre problems. Vallelunga showed that things could get worse — del Castello's engine expired on the warm-up lap and Dave was left on the grid with another crownwheel failure. At Pau, Dave crashed the March during the only dry practice session and failed to qualify, while a misfiring Heidegger put him at the back of the Jarama grid and then expired five laps from home, Dave being classified sixteenth.

With his future career at stake as every race went by, Dave had found these events profoundly worrying. Tyre development was proving to be a compromise affair, with Bridgestone attempting to service three different F2 chassis, while the Heidegger BMWs — generally regarded as fast but fragile — were having a particularly poor season. Prior to Donington, one of the three seats in the works March team, entrusted this year to Onyx Race Engineering, was on offer as its previous incumbent had run out of sponsorship funds. The Onyx Marches enjoyed the exclusive use of factory BMW engines as well as a contract with Michelin, makers of the best F2 rubber, and so Dave had decided to switch teams.

Dave had driven March-BMW No.3 for the first time earlier in the week at Goodwood, but now at Donington Dave is finding the car rolling and understeering, particularly through the faster corners, and seat and pedal adjustments are still called for. The second of the two half-hour periods on the track is further interrupted when the fuel pressure gauge pipe leaks petrol just behind Dave's head.

At the end of the day, it's decided to stiffen the front springs in an attempt to improve the car's handling: with Friday comprising just the two timed sessions to determine grid positions, it's important to use the unofficial Thursday sessions to sort the car as much as possible, so that it will be quick off the mark immediately the following day, before the road surface is slowed by a coating of rubber and oil. Several of the foreign drivers also use the day to acclimatize to a new circuit at racing speeds, but for Dave this is one weekend when he has the advantage of driving on a track with which he is already familiar.

Mint Intersport's vehicles in the paddock at Pau. Dave's Swift caravan is on the right.

Now armed with a works-backed Onyx March, Dave studies his lap times following a Donington practice session.

Although England is approaching mid-summer, Friday morning sees drizzle, mist and a strong cold wind enveloping the circuit, although a racing line is soon dried. Following the overnight adjustments to the March, Dave finds its tendency to roll has been eradicated, although the understeer persists. F2 regulations now permit only one set of qualifying tyres per car, and Dave comes in for his 45 minutes into the opening hour-long session. The Michelin radials have, in any case, required a different driving style to Intersport's Bridgestones, and now Dave

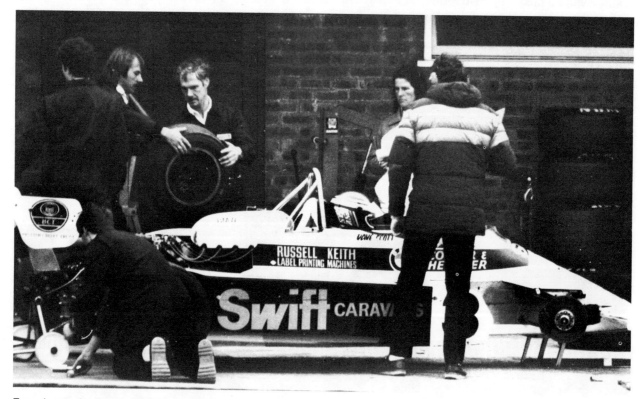

Tyre-change for Dave's March during practice.

belatedly discovers that the French qualifiers have only half the life of the Japanese company's equivalent rubber. After just three laps, the tyres are past their best, and Dave returns disconsolately to the pits for the remainder of the practice period. Despite this misjudgement, when the session times reach the pit lane, Dave's March has recorded the ninth quickest lap. Onyx Race Engineering's teamleader, Beppe Gabbiani, is third fastest behind the Ralt-Hondas of Jonathan Palmer and Mike Thackwell, while Dave's other team-mate, blond German Christian Danner, is down in twelfth position after experiencing engine problems.

Although the three men drive for the same team, Onyx's internal organisation (typical of most F2 set-ups) keeps each driver/car combination as a semi-independent operation. Each has their own manager — ex-Grand Prix driver Peter Gethin minding Gabbiani's Roloil-sponsored entry,

Trying for that quick lap: Dave is shown his lap time whilst Mike Earle looks on.

On the starting grid alongside Petit's Maurer.

March designer Ralph Bellamy overseeing Danner's efforts and team patron Mike Earle looking after Dave's requirements — and each a couple of mechanics, in Dave's case the young but well-versed Martin and Steve. Throughout practice, each driver is wrapped in a cocoon of concentration, discussing his car's characteristics with his three colleagues, going out onto the track for a few laps and then into the pits again to evaluate adjustments and suggest new measures, add fuel and have the all-important tyre temperatures taken, and then bolting on qualifiers and charging round for a quick time before the tyres destroy themselves, finally climbing out of the car at the session's end, clammy and red-faced with the effort, to disappear for a debriefing with his manager.

The weather remains bitterly cold for the second timed session. Martin and Steve have added more wing to the front and rear of Dave's March-BMW and lowered third gear, and after running intermediate tyres all round for most of the previous session, Dave is now armed with two hard tyres on the car's left side. Midway through the practice, Dave stops to fit stiffer springs, but these cause a loss of traction and increase the understeer, so before long March No.3 is back in the pit lane to have the original springs re-inserted. Dave returns to the circuit with his qualifiers fitted once more, albeit switched to different sides of the March. The ploy fails to come off and Dave is unable to improve on his earlier time, so he'll start tomorrow's race from the middle of the grid — two places behind an improved Danner. Apart from the first and last grid positions, practice ends with the entire field covered by just three seconds.

Dave spends the eve of the race hoping that this time the car will last. On his first race weekend with Onyx, he is understandably anxious to make a good impression. Some of his tension derives from a feeling that he has still to prove himself, for the 21-year-old's career to date has involved a rapid progression through the lower formulas with little opportunity to consolidate on his occasional successes.

After a year's break from karting, Dave had taken up Formula Ford racing with his own Royale, winning just one race (at Donington) in 18 months. An ambitious decision to move into F3 for 1981 saw Dave racing an Argo initially and matching or improving on the lap times set by its previous driver, the highly-rated Roberto Guerrero: a ground-effects Ralt RT3 was then purchased with which Dave frequently achieved front row grid times. In the last half of the season, Dave won two races and the media coverage which F3 attracts brought the 19-year-old the premier Grovewood Award as the year's most promising young British driver and a F1 testing contract with Lotus.

1982, however, was more down to earth. Dave had begun the season as a hot tip for the British F3 Championship, but the year proved a disappointment, Dave's driving lacking confidence as he found himself regularly beaten by Irishman Tommy Byrne, and his team losing its way amidst decisions to alter the make of engines in the back of the Ralt. Things managed to improve in the last months of the series, and Dave ended his F3 career with a win. So far, 1983 had been an even worse year, producing just the pole position at Silverstone, and so Dave is anxious to achieve that elusive good finish.

Following the unseasonal practice weather, raceday emerges bright and windless. For the morning untimed warm-up, all the Onyx Marches are fitted with hard tyres, the team doubting the wisdom of continuing with intermediates. At 10 o'clock — as the spectators still make their way round the circuit to their chosen viewing positions — Dave's car and the other F2 runners are released onto the track, all now in proposed race trim and on full tanks. After a few laps, the Onyx drivers come in to have the tyre temperatures checked. Dave also reports continuing understeer; Martin and Steve increase the front wing and stiffen the front anti-roll bar in a final attempt to be rid of the problem.

With the session over and the programme of supporting races underway, Dave reports that the understeer has worsened, so the adjustments to the front wing and anti-roll bar are reversed and two new dampers fitted to the March's rear. The effects of the understeer also mean that a new left front tyre is required, which Dave will have to scrub in on the warm-up lap immediately before the race starts.

Indeed, tyres now pose a problem for everyone, for the sun has come out and track temperatures have risen by over 10 degrees long after the teams have had to declare their final choice of race rubber. Seventy laps of Donington in such circumstances will entail the drivers racing with their tyres very much in mind, as they are likely to deteriorate substantially as the race wears on.

On their return to the startline, the cars are held by a red light. The green light comes on, the revs rise, the cars go into gear and the pack heads down towards the first corner. Dave — maintaining his tenth position — gets through in front of a nasty-looking accident as three cars touch and leave the track, one somersaulting into the crash barrier. All three drivers escape unhurt and remarkably composed, and, by the time the bend is cleared of debris, the F2 field has completed its first lap and is approaching once more. The Ralt-

Dave's March chasing the Maurers of Bellof and Acheson at Donington's Old Hairpin.

Hondas of Thackwell and Palmer lead from Gabbiani's March-BMW, then a small gap before Nannini (Minardi-BMW), Gartner (Spirit-BMW), Hoshino (March-BMW), Streiff (AGS-BMW), Danner (March-BMW), Petit (Maurer-BMW), Dave's March, Mansilla (March-BMW), Ferté (Martini-BMW) and the Maurers of Acheson and Bellof pass by in rapid succession.

In the course of the next few laps, Nannini and Gartner retire with mechanical maladies, Petit slows with loose bodywork and Mansilla — struggling with violent understeer in his March — manages to pass Dave, lying eighth now but with the hungry Maurers of Acheson and Bellof close behind and looking for a way by. Mansilla's blue March suddenly slows exiting the Old Hairpin, and Dave and Acheson collide at the next corner in their eagerness to take advantage of the situation; the Argentine keeps his position, while the March and Maurer retain their places despite the encounter. But Mansilla's oversteer worsens, so that his car is eventually overhauled before it stops for a change of tyres and drops out of the reckoning.

Up front, the Ralts continue to show the way from Gabbiani. Then the championship leader's exhaust pipe breaks, his BMW going offsong. On lap 14, the oil pump in the Onyx March fails, a fair stretch of the circuit receiving a slippery coating before the oil light in the cockpit flashes and Gabbiani coasts to a halt, his retirement elevating Streiff's AGS to third. The track marshals are slow to spot the dangerous road surface, and Dave almost spins off on his team-mate's oil, fighting to control the March as it takes to the grass, allowing Acheson and Bellof to finally nip past.

To make matters worse, as half-distance approaches the engine note on Dave's car turns to a drone as his exhaust breaks too. Danner's Onyx March suffers the same problem at about the same time, although he maintains his fifth place behind Japanese champion Hoshino for the remainder of the race. Four hundred revs down on the main straight, Dave drops further behind the two black Maurers, but he too soon realises the car can keep going after all. Indeed, as the German-backed cars suffer increasing understeer from worsening tyres and are held up by backmarkers, so Dave begins to catch up with them once more.

Each lap, Dave carefully brakes down from fifth to third gear at the end of the start/finish straight to enter Redgate — a corner which tightens on itself so that anyone leaving their braking too late will find themselves off the track on the exit — then moves back into fifth for the downward-sweeping Craner Curves, whose blind apex is soon accustomed to. The next corner, the right-hand Old Hairpin at the bottom of the hill, is one of Donington's most important bends and is taken very quickly in fourth gear. Dave then

107

changes up to fifth for the climb past Starkey's Bridge to McLeans — another important corner — where the March bears right in fourth gear, using up the full width of the road on exit from the constant radius curve. Dave continues in fourth up to Coppice, the trickiest of them all — a third-gear right-hander with obscured apex — which is best taken by quickly flicking the car into the bend, oversteering through the long curve and exiting in fourth. He then shifts into fifth for the 150mph straight under the Dunlop bridge towards the chicane. The s-bend is preceded by a small dip, where the March is taken down into third and then second gear for the chicane itself, Dave braking well in time for this the slowest section of the track, which takes the car back onto the start/finish straight.

Lap after such lap goes by, and each time Dave finds the lop-sided wing of Acheson's Maurer ahead tantalisingly nearer. The loss of revs caused by the March's broken exhaust has helped Dave conserve his tyres, whereas both Acheson's and Bellof's lap times are now two seconds off their best due to their tyres deteriorating on the hot track surface.

In the closing stages of the race, the spectators' attention is increasingly focussed on Dave's chase of the Maurers. Acheson's car is the worst affected by tyre trouble, and a few laps from home Dave passes the Ulsterman going into McLeans, the black car quickly dropping behind as Dave presses on, his sights now on Bellof. Dave closes inexorably, the highly-regarded German driver hampered by gearbox and braking problems. Just one lap from the chequered flag, Dave

squeezes the March past the Maurer under braking for Coppice to claim sixth place.

At the end of the race, the plaudits go to victor Jonathan Palmer, now heading the Ralt challenge to Gabbiani's (and March's) championship points lead. Although dismayed at the Italian's misfortune, Onyx are pleased with Danner's and Dave's fifth and sixth places given the exhaust pipe dramas. For Dave, his first championship point and the performance which went with it (recognised later in the afternoon by a Driver of the Day award) is vindication of his decision to compete in F2 in the first place. Not that he considers his Donington success as a comment on his erstwhile privateer efforts: Intersport's organisation was as strong as the Onyx effort and, given the right equipment and preferably some previous knowledge of the circuits involved, he remains convinced that a private team could still show strongly in F2.

As the mechanics begin packing the cars and equipment away into Onyx's huge transporter, Dave's raceday is still not over. First of all, he carries out his obligations to his current sponsors, by meeting with Swift Caravans' personnel and representatives from their finance company, and then Dave visits the March hospitality tent in the hope of making introductions which will lead to him retaining a works seat for 1984. When Dave leaves the circuit later on at the wheel of his BMW saloon, his mind is already on the hovercraft journey to Belgium in two days' time, when Onyx will be carrying out tyre tests at Zolder — the scene of another F2 Championship race weekend later in the season.

Dave's determined drive brings him his first finish in the Championship points.

8 The Champions

H. 12323

Although a graded driver by the time the European Championship was introduced and therefore ineligible for championship points, **Jochen Rindt** was regarded as the undisputed King of F2 between 1967 and 1970, winning a total of 23 races during this period.

Following some saloon car and Formula Junior competition, it was F2 which brought Jochen into the motor racing limelight when, in 1964, the German orphan (who, raised by grandparents in Graz, always considered himself an Austrian) sank all his assets into the purchase of a Brabham-Cosworth to compete against the world's top drivers.

He put on impressive performances at the Nürburgring and Mallory Park before winning the Crystal Palace Whit Monday event after an epic duel with ex-World Champion Graham Hill. By the end of the year, the dour-faced Rindt had made his F1 début for Rob Walker, while 1965 saw his biggest sportscar success — a win at Le Mans in a Ferrari 250LM shared with Masten Gregory.

Despite his increasing dominance of F2, where his determined, press-on style of driving and brilliant car control gained him legions of fans, success eluded him in F1, although he was regarded as the fastest Grand Prix driver of all. For three seasons, he struggled with Coopers, managing a third place in the 1966 World Drivers' Championship. Jochen then joined Brabham-Repco for a disappointing year. His first F1 win finally came at the end of 1969, when he won the American Grand Prix for Lotus after a problem ridden season with the Norfolk team — including a serious accident in Spain in which his jaw was broken.

By now a resident of Switzerland with his wife and daughter, Jochen was one of the first European drivers to build a business career around his motor racing exploits, and it was only the combination of attractive financial terms and the promise of a revolutionary new car — the Lotus 72 — which persuaded him to remain with Lotus for 1970. Rindt went on to win the Monaco, Dutch, French, British and German Grands Prix, and the World Championship title beckoned at Monza. Here, however, his luck ran out, the Lotus crashing inexplicably at the fast Parabolica Curve in practice and Jochen dying from his injuries. With his rivals unable to better his points score in the remaining races, Jochen Rindt became motor racing's first posthumous World Champion. The King was dead — long live the King.

Jochen Rindt.

● Right from the start, people reckoned **Jacky Ickx** would become a World Champion. A celebrity in Belgium at the age of 18 following two years of motobike successes, Jacky switched to four wheels and had already twice won the notorious Spa 24 Hours saloon car race before Ken Tyrell picked him for F3 in 1966.

The following year, the fresh-faced 22-year-old won the first European F2 Championship, finished in the points on his F1 début for Cooper-Maserati and was snapped up by Ferrari for 1968. Piloting the red cars with a mature confidence which belied his years, Jacky won the wet French Grand Prix and came fourth in the World Drivers' Championship despite breaking a leg in a crash in Canada. During the next two seasons (1969 with Brabham, 1970 back with Ferrari), the Belgian scored more Grand Prix victories, but had to settle for runner-up championship position on both occasions.

Thereafter, Ickx's chances of a world title appeared to have gone. His F1 opportunities dwindled: although his virtuosity continued to shine through on occasions (his manoeuvre past Lauda's Ferrari on the outside of a rain-soaked Paddock Bend to win the 1974 Race of Champions for Lotus perhaps being the best-known example), Jacky spent most of the remainder of his F1 career driving for minor league outfits, and he failed to make the most of his opportunities with better-financed teams like Lotus and Ligier. In 1979, he effectively retired from Grand Prix racing.

But Jacky had another card up his sleeve. Since 1967, the Belgian had built a considerable reputation in sportscar racing, initially with John Wyer's organisation (winning Le Mans in 1969 and 1975) and Ferrari (Ickx's six wins in the 312P giving Maranello the World Sportscar Championship in 1972). Ickx was then invited to head Porsche's sportscar efforts, his 1976 and 1977 victories for the German firm at the Sarthe bringing him a personal tally of three consecutive wins at Le Mans. An historic fifth triumph in the French classic continued to elude him, Jacky coming home second in 1978 and in 1980, although the Belgian won the lucrative CanAm sportscar series in 1979 at the wheel of a Lola-Chevrolet.

FISA's attempts to revitalise sportscar racing in 1981 and the consequent re-entry of Porsche saw Ickx come out of retirement to lead their team once more — and Jacky scored his unique fifth Le Mans win partnered by Derek Bell in a Porsche 936. The victory obtained, Jacky decided to continue competing in sportscar racing, for which a World Sportscar Drivers' Championship had now been constituted. Porsche extended their backing the following year to enable Ickx to press for

championship honours — and a brilliant drive in half-light at the final Brands Hatch round saw Jacky defeat the Lancia of championship rival Riccardo Patrese to finally obtain his World Champion title after all.

Jacky Ickx.

● When, after achieving 11 national motorbike championships, the diminutive Frenchman **Jean-Pierre Beltoise** decided to turn his attention to car racing, he could hardly have known that he would become France's first racing driver hero for a decade and a crucial figure in his country's motor racing renaissance. For France had launched no major racing initiative since the ill-fated Gordini efforts in the mid-1950s, nor had there been a top-line driver regularly upholding the tricolour in international competition since Jean Behra's death on the Avus circuit in 1959.

Jean-Pierre began his four-wheeled career in sportscar racing with René Bonnet — a career which almost ended at the 1964 Rheims 12-Hour Race, when a bad accident put him out of racing for several months and left him with a permanent limp and a weak left arm. Beltoise returned at the wheel of a F3 Matra (the missile company having taken over the Bonnet firm), winning the 1965 French F3 Championship and the prestigious Monaco F3 race the following year.

With the French Government and its associated petrol company Elf keen to see France re-establish its motor sport prestige, Matra and Jean-Pierre were chosen in 1967 to spearhead the French comeback, the combination taking the European F2 Championship and entering F1. The partnership (including occasional loans to Ken Tyrell's Matra-Ford set-up) lasted four more seasons, the gritty Jean-Pierre taking the V12-engined car to second place at the wet 1968 Dutch Grand Prix and retiring whilst leading the 1970 French Grand Prix; and finishing second in the 1969 French Grand Prix and almost winning that year's Italian Grand Prix in the Ford-engined MS80. 1971 was clouded by the Frenchman being held responsible for the death of Ignazio Giunti during an Argentine sportscar race, and at the end of the year he was dropped by Matra, signing for the Marlboro-backed BRM team for 1972.

At a rain-soaked Monte Carlo that year, Jean-Pierre drove magnificently to dominate and win the Monaco Grand Prix — his only Grand Prix victory, for the remainder of the season held no such glories. Beltoise stayed with the erratically-run BRM set-up for two more years, being overshadowed by team mates Lauda and Regazzoni in 1973, but finishing a strong second in the new P201 at the 1974 South African Grand Prix — the car's most competitive showing.

In 1973, Jean-Pierre had shared a Matra MS670 at Le Mans with brother-in-law François Cevert, retiring whilst leading, and for 1975 Beltoise turned his attention to sportscar racing for former F2 driver Guy Ligier: he also assisted with early development of the first F1 Ligier car, only to be passed over in favour of new French hope Jacques Laffite once the machine was raceworthy. Beltoise's international racing days were over, and he resigned himself to driving in occasional French sportscar and saloon events, where he is still a popular participant.

- **Johnny Servoz-Gavin** sped across the motor racing firmament like a brief shooting star. Fired by two passions — skiing and motor racing — Johnny was pronounced "too wild" after an initial racing driving course at the Winfield Magny-Cours school, but, undeterred, the handsome blond Frenchman turned to navigating in rallies and drove in occasional club events while he saved for a F3 car. In 1965, he purchased a Brabham and a tent in which to sleep at race meetings and managed to finish fourth in the French F3 Championship — good enough to be awarded a works Matra drive for the following season.

By 1968, Johnny had become somewhat eclipsed by the other Matra regulars Beltoise, Jaussaud and Pescarolo, but he earned renewed attention with a rousing drive to fourth place in a F2 Matra at the non-championship Madrid Grand Prix: the performance led to his F2 Championship-winning ride in Ken Tyrell's Matra the following year. Standing in for an injured Jackie Stewart, Servoz-Gavin also made an exhilarating F1 début for Tyrell at Monaco, setting fastest practice time in the Matra-Ford and leading the Grand Prix until he brushed a chicane and damaged the car's suspension. Second place at the Italian Grand Prix and sixth with the uncompetitive 4-wheel-drive Matra MS84 in Canada secured a full-time F1 contract with Tyrell for 1970, but the Frenchman surprised the motor racing world by announcing his immediate retirement from competition driving early that same season. "Fear has won me over," he said, "I haven't got any more confidence".

Jean-Pierre Beltoise.

Johnny Servoz-Gavin.

111

● **Gianclaudio 'Clay' Regazzoni** was always a battler. Born in Lugano (in the Italian-speaking part of Switzerland) the son of a coachbuilder, Clay spent a couple of years competing in hillclimbs — circuit racing being banned in Switzerland — before completing a racing drivers' course at Montlhéry, France, and beginning F3 racing. He rapidly gained a reputation as a wild charger and uncompromising opponent, joining the works Tecno team in 1967 and punting off two competitors at Hockenheim to win the European Team Trophy for Switzerland. Regazzoni then entered F2 with the Bologna firm, winning the European Championship in 1970 — when he also made an impressive mid-season start in F1 with Ferrari, finishing third in the World Driver's Championship and instigating an adoring relationship with Italian race fans by winning their Grand Prix for Maranello. The Swiss remained with Ferrari for a further two seasons, but the 312B-2/71 proved a troublesome car and Regazzoni grew more accident-prone before Ferrari temporarily withdrew from motor racing in 1972.

A miserably uncompetitive season with BRM followed, Clay being fortunate to survive a fiery crash at the South African Grand Prix, when Mike Hailwood pulled him unconscious from the wreckage. Back with Ferrari for 1974, Regazzoni showed he'd lost none of his old aggression, winning the German Grand Prix and finishing second in four other World Championship rounds and only being beaten to the title at the final race by Emerson Fittipaldi. Next year, he won the Italian Grand Prix once more, and provided excellent support to team-mate Niki Lauda in his successful bid for the championship, while in 1974 Clay won the inaugural Long Beach Grand Prix and helped Ferrari secure the Constructors' Championship.

Parting from Ferrari in 1977, Clay spent two seasons with the uncompetitive Ensign and Shadow teams before his career was resuscitated by Frank Williams' decision that the Swiss should partner Alan Jones in his Saudia-backed cars. The Williams-Ford FW07 proved a front-runner immediately, Regazzoni powering through from 16th grid position at Monte Carlo to finish just 0.4 seconds behind winner Jody Scheckter, and at Silverstone it was Clay who brought the Williams team its first Grand Prix victory after ten years in the wilderness.

The announcement that he was to be replaced at Williams' for 1980 by Carlos Reutemann came as a surprise to many: the Swiss joined the Ensign team once more, on this occasion with more promising machinery. It all came to naught, however, at Long Beach, when the car's brake pedal snapped on the circuit's main straight — the Ensign catapulted head-on into

crash barriers, causing severe injuries to Regazzoni's spine and legs. The chances of Clay being able to walk again were pronounced slim, and suddenly the old campaigner had a longer and slower battle to fight.

Clay Regazzoni.

● With his similarly fast, confident and often sideways style of driving, **Ronnie Peterson** was the natural successor to Jochen Rindt's unofficial King of F2 title.

His father having raced 500cc cars, Ronnie took up motorbike and kart racing before graduating to Swedish F3 with a home-built car at the age of 22. Two years later, driving a Tecno, the blond Swede scooped his country's F3 Championship, and the following year (1969) he raced further afield, enjoying numerous victories including the Monaco F3 event.

At the end of that season, Peterson débuted March's F3 car (the first model to be produced by the Bicester-based concern), and the company arranged F1 and F2 drives for him for 1970 in their tricky 701 and 702 designs. Next season was more successful, the Swede taking the F2 title and showing strongly in F1, where he lost the Italian Grand Prix to Peter Gethin's BRM by one hundredth of a second! In 1972, the futuristic-looking March 721X proved a design disaster, and Ronnie ended the Grand Prix season at the wheel of the company's successful F2 chassis, fitted with ballast for F1. He then moved to Lotus as joint number one with

World Champion Emerson Fittipaldi, where he confirmed himself as the fastest F1 driver of all, and after narrowly losing his home Grand Prix, won at France, Austria and Italy – the latter victory effectively ending his team-mate's chances of retaining the Drivers' Championship, the title going to Jackie Stewart once more. The following year, the Swede's brilliant driving took the ageing Lotus 72 to further triumphs in the Monaco, French and Italian Grands Prix, but the difficulties which Lotus were encountering in producing a competitive successor prompted Peterson to return to March in 1976 in a straight exchange for compatriot Gunnar Nilsson.

March, however, continued to suffer extensive reliability problems, Ronnie's only success being a further Italian Grand Prix win, by which time he'd already decided to drive the Tyrell P34 six-wheeler in 1977. The car failed to realise its early promise, the Swede suffering a poor season in which he was often outpaced by team-mate Patrick Depailler.

For 1978, then, Peterson returned to Lotus – although this time as number two to Mario Andretti. The ground effects-based Lotus 79s dominated Grand Prix racing that year. Ronnie revived his reputation with a scintillating last-lap victory in the South African Grand Prix, and went on to back up Andretti in 1–2 results in Belgium, Spain, France and Holland, often seeming to have plenty of speed in hand on the American. A further win at the Austrian Grand Prix meant that the Swede went to Monza as Andretti's only rival for the World Championship, although it was anticipated that Ronnie (who had signed to lead McLaren in 1979) would continue to follow team orders and shadow Andretti to the flag if

Ronnie Peterson.

necessary. In the event, a badly-organised start led to a chain-reaction accident at the first corner in which Peterson and Vittorio Brambilla were both badly injured. The popular Swede succumbed the following morning, to the shock of the motor racing world and in particular to Mario Andretti, who – in a repeat of fellow American Phil Hill's experience at Monza 17 years earlier – had gone on to win both the Grand Prix and the championship following the fatal accident to his team-mate.

● One of motorbike racing's greats (he won no less than nine motorcycling World Championships between 1961 and '68), when **Mike Hailwood** expressed a desire to compete on four wheels, he was immediately welcomed into the upper echelons of motor racing, driving a Lotus-BRM for Reg Parnell in 1964 Grands Prix. However, the car proved outdated and unreliable, and Mike continued to concentrate on bikes, accepting the occasional sportscar drive until he announced his retirement from motorcycle racing in 1968.

For the next three years, Hailwood competed regularly in British F5000 single-seater racing, signing for Lola in 1969 and 1970 (and netting two wins), and then driving for fellow motorcyclist John Surtees to finish runner-up in the 1971 Championship with four race victories to his credit. By now, the Oxford-born racer had developed an impressive all-round ability and, given the opportunity to drive a F1 Surtees at the Italian Grand Prix, led the slipstreaming race on several occasions before finishing fourth. Next year, Mike agreed to do both F2 and F1 for the Edenbridge concern, his Hart-powered F2 Championship win marking the peak of his four-wheeled achievements, while in F1 he managed a couple of second places. He remained with Surtees for 1973, which marked the start of the team's decline in competitiveness, and continued his sportscar association with John Wyer (Hailwood had finished third at Le Mans for him in 1969), winning the Spa 1000 Km in a Mirage-Ford with Derek Bell. His bravery in rescuing Clay Regazzoni following a crash at the South African GP resulted in his being awarded the George Medal.

The following season, the Yardley cosmetics firm decided to end their support for BRM and to sponsor instead a singleton McLaren-Ford run from the works. Hailwood landed the drive and began the season strongly, only to crash heavily in the German Grand Prix on the Nürburgring, smashing one of his legs so badly that he decided to retire altogether from racing and emigrate to New Zealand.

However, by 1978, Mike had grown bored with his inactivity and competed in some Australian saloon car races before making a highly-publicised return to the Isle of Man (scene of 12 previous TT victories) to add a further motorcycling World Championship to his name by winning an event for F1 bike racers. He returned to live in England and won a further TT the following year, but the talented all-rounder now admitted to having become tired of racing, and he forsook the tracks to run a Birmingham motorcycle dealership. In March, 1981, whilst out driving on the road, his car and a lorry collided, the accident tragically claiming the lives of Hailwood and his two children.

Mike Hailwood.

● **Jean-Pierre Jarier** has been one of motor racing's great disappointments, never living up to the promise he showed during his dominant F2 Championship season with March-BMW in 1973.

An economics graduate, the baby-faced Parisian started racing Renault saloons before moving up the motor racing ladder by competing in Formule France and F3, his natural flair and Shell sponsorship taking him into F2 and even F1 as early as 1971, when he brought home a privately-entered March in 12th place in the Italian Grand Prix. Two years later, as well as landing the championship-winning F2 March drive, Jarier piloted the singleton works F1 car in several Grands Prix, his best showing in an uncompetitive machine being sixth place prior to retirement in Belgium.

For 1974, Jean-Pierre signed to partner Pete Revson in the UOP Shadow team, which was badly affected by Revson's death at the start of the season when testing at Kyalami: the best result for the Frenchman, now promoted to team leader, was third at Monte Carlo. Jarier remained with Shadow for two more seasons, and in both 1975 and '76 caused a sensation by proving fastest of all in the opening South American rounds. But the car usually failed to finish, and eventually Jean-Pierre's disillusionment would become reflected in his driving. In the latter season, he failed even to score a World Championship point: dropped by Shadow, he was picked up for 1977 by the new ATS team (running the previous year's F1 Penske-Fords). He managed sixth place at the Long Beach Grand Prix, only to become increasingly half-hearted once more as the season wore on without further results being achieved.

For the final Grand Prix that year, Jarier found himself in the second Ligier-Matra seat, but no option was exercised for 1978, when the Frenchman's racing was largely confined to sportscar drives with Alpine Renault and the CanAm Shadow. However, following Ronnie Peterson's death at Monza, Jean-Pierre was offered the vacant Lotus 79 seat for the last two Grands Prix of the season, and, revelling at the opportunity of driving a proven race-winner, he once more displayed his exceptional talent, setting fastest lap in a classic drive through the field at Watkins Glen and then attaining pole

Jean-Pierre Jarier.

position and a clear lead at the Canadian Grand Prix until two-thirds distance, when an oil leak caused his retirement.

After such performances, Jarier's F1 future was assured once again, the Parisian enjoying his best-ever Grand Prix season the following year with Tyrell, finishing third in South Africa and Britain. Following less success in 1980, Ken Tyrell opted for a change of drivers, and an upset Jean-Pierre was left without a regular ride until mid-season when he joined the struggling Osella set-up. This rickety partnership lasted until the end of 1982, when the Frenchman deemed the car too dangerous to drive further! Fortunately, his decision coincided with a vacancy for the number one Ligier drive, and so Jean-Pierre excitedly joined the French team. 1983, however, proved to be the year when turbocharged engines began to dominate F1 racing and, stuck with the normally-aspirated Ford unit, Jarier once more remained frustrated.

● The motor racing career of **Patrick Depailler** always seemed to be interrupted by accidents at crucial stages.

Born in Clermont Ferrand, Patrick began motorbike racing at the age of 18 as a protégé of Jean-Pierre Beltoise, himself a bike racer at the time. Following completion of a race drivers' course at the well-known Winfield School at Magny-Cours — where Depailler finished second in the end-of-term Volant Shell awards to one François Cevert — Beltoise helped him secure a three-year contract with the Elf-backed Alpine Renault team as mechanic and test driver. Patrick began a number of F3 successes for the équipe at the 1976 Paris Grand Prix at Montlhéry.

In 1970, Depailler entered F2 with the all-French Pygmée effort, but the team ran out of funds and Patrick returned to F3, winning the French Championship for Alpine Renault the following season. His career continued to prosper in 1972, Patrick winning the F3 Monaco race and beginning a concentrated effort in F2 which was to secure him the European Championship two years later. With the assistance of sponsors Elf, he also guest-drove with Ken Tyrell's F1 team at the French and American Grands Prix. Depailler was lined up for further Tyrell drives at the 1973 Canadian and American races, but he injured himself fooling around on a motorbike and could not take part after all, his relationship with the team threatened.

However, Cevert's death at Watkins Glen and Jackie Stewart's retirement from racing meant that Tyrell found himself with no contracted drivers for 1974 and Depailler became Elf's best prospect for a French World Champion, so he joined the team after all as number two to Jody Scheckter. Patrick's best results were second

places behind his South African team-mate at the 1975 and '76 Swedish Grands Prix, latterly in the P34 six-wheeler. Following a lean 1977 with a muted Ronnie Peterson as team leader, the Frenchman was given the number one Tyrell seat and a new, conventional four-wheeler: after being deprived of the chequered flag by Peterson's Lotus on the last lap at Kyalami, Depailler finally made it to the winner's rostrum with a victory at Monte Carlo.

Thereafter, the car failed to develop competitively, and for 1979 Patrick transferred to Ligier, who were changing from Matra to Ford engines and wanted someone with experience of Cosworth power to partner their established driver, Jacques Laffite. There was considerable needle between the two French aces, Laffite winning the Argentine and Brazilian Grands Prix and Depailler coming home first in Spain and leading comfortably in Belgium before crashing. Away from the circuits, Patrick continued to lead an adventurous lifestyle, and this time a serious hang-gliding accident dashed his World Championship hopes by putting him out of racing for the remainder of the year. Guy Ligier angrily terminated his contract.

Although still far from fit, Depailler was snapped up for the following year by Alfa Romeo,

Patrick Depailler.

who were anxious to acquire an experienced test driver to sort their promising 179 V12. Patrick put a lot of effort into developing the car, which gained in competitiveness but continued to suffer from poor reliability. Onlookers felt that success was just around the corner, but, testing at Hockenheim prior to the German Grand Prix, Depailler's Alfa suddenly veered off-course at the extremely fast Ostkurve: at the speed he was travelling, the driver had no time to attempt to correct the car before it plunged into an unprotected barrier, and this time there would be no return for the Frenchman, for he was killed instantly.

● 1975 European Champion **Jacques Laffite** worked his way from the bottom to the top of motor racing, his original involvement in the sport being as race mechanic on Jean-Pierre Jabouille's F3 cars in the late 1960s, when he also worked at the Winfield racing drivers' school at his home town of Magny-Cours. In 1968, aged 24, Laffite himself began racing in F3, although he soon switched to the cheaper Formule Renault, in which he became French Champion in his fourth season of competition. This success brought BP France backing for a works Martini drive, Jacques enjoying a phenomenal 1973, with victory in the French F3 Championship and the important Monaco race and fourth position in the British F3 Championship despite having to miss several rounds because of clashing commitments. At one stage in the season, Laffite went 10 races without defeat, and BP were happy to continue supporting him in F2 from 1974.

The rugged Frenchman also drove one of Frank Williams's Iso Marlboros in the last five Grands Prix of the year, doing sufficiently well in the uncompetitive car to obtain a further contract for 1975, when his best result was a determined drive to second place at the Nüburgring. As well as clinching the F2 Championship, Jacques partnered Arturo Merzario to three sportscar victories for Alfa Romeo and tested France's new Grand Prix contender, the Ligier-Matra.

Chosen as their singleton driver for 1976, Jacques stayed faithful to the Ligier team for seven seasons. Forging a strong partnership with patron Guy Ligier, he soon established himself as a persistent, gritty racer, putting in several sterling performances which culminated in the first all-French World Championship Grand Prix win at Sweden in 1977. After a less successful season in 1978, Ligier jettisoned the Matra V12 engine, switched to Cosworth power and added Patrick Depailler as second driver. The Ford-engined JS11 proved extremely competitive, Laffite winning the first two Grands Prix in Argentina and Brazil and emerging as a leading championship contender before the car was wrongly modified in

mid-season and lost its superiority, Jacques finishing fourth in the World Championship he had earlier been tipped to win. In 1980, the Frenchman led a number of Grands Prix only to retire for one reason or another: he did win the German round following Alan Jones's retirement, and again finished fourth in the Championship.

The following year, Ligier linked up with Talbot, involving a move back to the Matra engine. Although off the pace at the start of the season, the JS17 was rapidly developed by Jacques and brother-in-law Jean-Pierre Jabouille, the popular Laffite taking two titanic victories at the daunting Österreichring and a sodden Montreal and going to the last round at Las Vegas with an outside chance of the World Championship. Tyre trouble prevented his finishing higher than sixth, and Jacques was fourth in the championship table for the third year running!

Laffite and Ligier had a dreadful time in 1982, Jacques' best placing being third at Austria, and he was happy next season to rejoin Frank Williams whose now-successful team also boasted World Champion Keke Rosberg. The Cosworth-powered FW08C, however, was no match for the turbocharged runners, and Jacques had to wait until the season's end before the team acquired the Honda turbo engine.

Jacques Laffite.

● Born in the Auvergne, France, in 1942, **Jean-Pierre Jabouille**, who became the epitome of the modern race development driver, began racing at the age of 23 with a Renault 8 Gordini saloon. In 1967, he competed in the French F3 Championship, winning a round at Rheims, and did not move up to F2 until 1972, by which time he had finished runner-up in the F3 category for three consecutive years. Jean-Pierre displayed sound mechanical and engineering knowledge, to the extent that Elf were happy to have him construct a F2 car in the fuel company's name when his employers, Alpine, turned their attentions to sportscar racing. It was the engineering abilities behind his 1976 European Championship success and his sportscar experience with Matra and Alpine from 1973–74 which led to Jabouille being chosen to assist the Renault company's campaign to win Le Mans: victory was eventually achieved in 1978 (by Jean-Pierre Jaussaud and Didier Pironi), Jabouille having played a major role in the team's engineering and development activities.

The lanky Frenchman's Grand Prix début occurred in the 1975 French Grand Prix through an Elf-assisted drive with Tyrell, but his involvement with Renault led to him being the natural choice to develop the firm's ambitious turbocharged F1 project. Sole team driver in 1977 and '78, Jabouille achieved progress with the car although reliability problems persisted. By 1979, Jean-Pierre (now joined by René Arnoux) was able to place the Renault on pole position for four

Jean-Pierre Jabouille.

Grands Prix and took an emotional all-French win at his home event – his only finish in the points all season, as the car still proved fragile. The next year, the improvement in the Renaults was more marked, and although Jabouille spent much of the time overshadowed by his spirited team-mate, he nevertheless scored an impressive victory at Austria over Alan Jones's Williams.

Unfortunately, Jean-Pierre's Renault crashed at high speed at Canada following a suspension failure and both the Frenchman's legs were very badly broken. He had already decided to leave Renault at the season's end to join his brother-in-law and former mechanic Jacques Laffite at Ligier. However, after a handful of races, Jean-Pierre sadly concluded that his injuries would prevent him from remaining a competitive Grand Prix driver, and he retired from racing to become instead Ligier's test driver and development engineer, contributing greatly to Laffite's victories in the JS17 later that season. When Laffite left Ligier in 1983, Jean-Pierre stayed on, putting his engineering knowledge to good use on their F1 and Indycar projects.

● As is the case with many of today's racing drivers, **René Arnoux** started in motor sport by taking up kart racing. He drove karts for six years from the age of 12, studied mechanical engineering and then worked in a garage preparing rally cars, before completing a race drivers' course at the Winfield School – next year (1973), he was France's Formule Renault Champion! Instead of proceeding up the conventional ladder into Formule Super Renault, the ambitious young Frenchman decided instead to contest the European F5000 Championship at the wheel of a Shell Sport-backed McLaren M19: the car proved uncompetitive and was jettisoned in mid-season in favour of F2 races with an Elf-sponsored Martini. Despite his shyness off the track and his lack of success on it, Arnoux impressed many with his driving ability, and was even awarded a F1 testing contract with Lotus, although it was never taken up by the Norfolk team.

For 1975, René moved back to Super Renault, establishing himself as a young charger and winning the championship and a Martini-Renault drive in F2 the following year. With the European Championship won in 1977, Arnoux and Tico Martini set their sights on continuing their successful partnership in F1, but the underfinanced Martini-Ford project almost bankrupted the tiny French company and Arnoux was unable to make much of an impression.

However, at the wheel of a Surtees in the Canadian and American (East) Grands Prix at the end of the year, René put in some tigerish performances and – with Surtees pulling out of Grand Prix racing at the close of the season – was snapped up by Renault for 1979. Arnoux immediately proved highly competitive, setting fastest practice times in Austria and Holland and finishing second at Silverstone and Watkins Glen, although his most sensational drive came at Dijon, where he joined in a frantic last-lap duel with fellow fighter Gilles Villeneuve to finish in third place.

In 1980, Arnoux won two consecutive early Grands Prix in Brazil and South Africa to overshadow team leader Jabouille and stake a claim to the World Championship, but mechanical troubles and tyre problems later in the season put paid to his hopes. A somewhat inconsistent driver, René then had a couple of lean years at Renault, his new team-mate Alain Prost usurping his place as the company's main hope for World Championship success. Following Arnoux's refusal to cede victory of the 1982 French Grand Prix to Prost, thereby ending his team-mate's championship chances, relations between René and Renault soured and he eagerly accepted an offer to drive for Ferrari in 1983. At Maranello, he continued on his individual way, overtaking 'team-mate' Patrick Tambay in the race for championship honours (and a 1984 Ferrari seat) by winning the Canadian, German and Dutch Grands Prix, only to cede the drivers' title to Piquet at the final race.

● The son of a Brescia farmer, **Bruno Giacomelli** soon developed an interest in all things mechanical: after studying to become a draughtsman, Bruno undertook a series of jobs and, by remaining at his parents' home, was able to save some money to go motor racing, beginning in Formula Ford after completing a racing drivers' course at Monza. These activities were interrupted by National Service, and Giacomelli recommenced racing driving in Formula Italia, winning the Italian Championship in 1975 with a self-prepared car. Bruno decided to drive a F3 March in Italy the following year, but, after meeting March Sales Manager Sandro Angelari during a trip to Bicester to buy some spares, found himself offered the works car in British F3: he went on to win both the Shell F3 Championship and the important Monaco F3 event.

Beginning 1977 with an Italian-backed semi-works March in F2, Bruno was drawn into the works team when the venture folded in mid-season. The following year, he dominated the European Championship with March, but his few drives for McLaren in F1 were less successful and he seemed unlikely to secure a further F1 drive until he was taken on by Alfa Romeo to head the firm's comeback to Grand Prix racing. Giacomelli remained loyal to the team for four years. Although their efforts did not meet with much success, he led sensationally the 1980 American (East) Grand Prix until electrical problems intervened and put in

René Arnoux.

Bruno Giacomelli.

some strong performances in the Tasman series that winter.

At the end of 1982, overshadowed at Alfa Romeo by the up and coming Andrea de Cesaris, Bruno moved across to the turbocharged but struggling Toleman team, which contained several of the personnel from his 1978 March season. Success continued to elude the Italian, whose approach to racing seemed to lack any great desire to improve things when stuck in uncompetitive machinery.

● 1979 European Championship winner **Marc Surer** took up kart racing at an early age and won the Swiss Kart Championship by the time he was 20. Following a course at the Jim Russell Österreichring School, Marc — helped by a German benefactor he'd met there — began Formula Vee racing, winning his first race in the rain over a lap ahead of the other runners and finishing second in the 1974 German Championship. The following year, his sponsor was unable to continue his support, so Surer remained in Formula Vee, although he did manage a couple of F3 outings towards the end of the season, leading on both occasions. With financial backing still unforthcoming, he had to turn down the chance of a works F3 March drive for 1976, and instead prepared and drove his own shoestring F3 effort, finishing fifth in the European series and second in the German Championship.

Surer's career was to be marked by such poorly-financed ventures, but in 1977 fortune smiled on him when BMW offered him a car in the German Group 5 contests, the rapid Swiss enjoying a fierce rivalry on the tracks with fellow BMW junior Eddie Cheever. Marc also attempted a full F2 season, but again suffered from insufficient resources. With continued BMW backing, however, a works March F2 drive was obtained in 1978, Marc playing best man to Giacomelli prior to claiming the championship in his own right the following year.

Offered the F1 Ensign seat for the remainder of 1979, Surer failed to qualify the uncompetitive car at Monza, but finally made his F1 début for the team at the American (East) Grand Prix. For 1980, Marc signed to drive the German-backed ATS, only to break both his legs quite severely during practice for the South African Grand Prix: the Swiss returned to the cockpit in mid-season, but soon lost the confidence of impatient team owner Gunter Schmid. Despite his F1 problems, Surer proved his worth with strong showings against his fellow Grand Prix drivers in the equally-matched BMW Procar series held during 1979 and '80.

Next year, Marc moved back to Ensign and did well to finish in the points in two World Championship rounds: however, Mo Nunn's team could not afford the testing needed to race

develop the car, let alone continue to run an unsponsored driver, so the association ended after Monaco. The Swiss was fortunate to pick up a vacancy at Theodore, but this was another struggling team and the remainder of the season held no glories, Surer managing to augment his living with occasional F2 and saloon car appearances.

His earlier performances had caused sufficient impression for him to be offered the number one Arrows drive for 1982, but the year began badly with another big crash at Kyalami causing further injuries to Surer's legs. The Arrows was never a front runner, although Marc managed a couple of placings once he'd recovered. 1983 witnessed a change of fortunes for the team, which emerged as one of the quickest Ford-powered combinations in a year largely dominated by turbocharged cars: the determined Swiss again made the most of the machinery at his disposal.

Marc Surer.

● **Brian Henton's** gritty individualism is perhaps a legacy of his father's death in an industrial explosion when Brian was just 10 years old. Taking on the role of family provider, Henton left school at 15, initially to begin an apprenticeship at the same factory where his father had worked, but was soon involved in wheeler-dealing used cars: with the apprenticeship completed, Brian and a friend set up their own engineering firm, which grew to become the biggest manufacturer of portable road signs in Britain.

The Derbyshire lad had always harboured dreams of becoming a top-line motor racing driver, and his business success meant that he was able to start financing his racing career from the age of 22. After competing in Formula Vee (winning the British Championship in 1971) and Formula Atlantic, Henton moved into F3, doing sufficiently well to secure a works March drive in 1974 and win two major championships. The following year, he began his personal flag-waving assault on F2 — a six-year obsession which, with assistance from Tom Wheatcroft and Toleman along the way, finally saw him crowned European Champion.

His F1 career has been more of an up-and-down affair. In 1975, Brian ran number two to Ronnie Peterson at Lotus, but — always the individual — Brian found it difficult to adapt to the team's ways, asked to be released from his 3-year contract with Lotus and then sank money from his motor businesses into running his own F1 March. Life as a F1 privateer proved unsuccessful, however, and so he turned his back on Grand Prix racing to concentrate on F2 — his favourite formula.

Following their domination of F2, Henton and Toleman moved together into F1 for 1981, running a turbocharged development of the Hart F2 engine. The effort was an extremely ambitious one unlikely to gain immediate success, but the lengthy saga of non-qualifications throughout the year was more than anyone had bargained for, and Brian lost his place when it was decided to put

120   *Brian Henton.*

Teo Fabi into one of the Italian-sponsored cars for 1982. Marc Surer's accident at Kyalami that year enabled the stocky Henton to step into the Arrows team, where he covered sufficiently well to be offered the number two Tyrell drive on a race-by-race basis once Surer had recovered. Driving a car considerably heavier than that of his team leader Michele Alboreto, Brian nevertheless set fastest lap at the British Grand Prix and drove a furious race to fifth place in Austria. But he didn't command the sponsorship to remain with Tyrell for the following season, and plans to establish his own F1 effort once more failed to materialise.

● A shy Warwickshire man, **Geoff Lees** was initially connected with motor racing as a mechanic, but sprang to prominence in 1975 when he won no less than three major British Formula Ford championships.

Lack of funds prevented him from competing in a full season of F3 races, so Geoff could frustratedly only manage occasional one-off drives until 1978, when Midlands businessman Jack Kallay entered him in several British F1 Championship and F2 races, Lees proving immediately competitive in both categories, although a hard charger prone to off-track excursions. The following year, Lees drove a Lola T333CS for Count van der Straten's VDS CanAm team, finishing third in the sportscar series. In Europe, further one-off drives continued — Geoff deputised for an ill Jean-Pierre Jarier at the German Grand Prix, bringing his Tyrell home in seventh place; caused a sensation at a televised British F1 event at Silverstone by keeping an outdated Wolf WR4 amongst the skirted race leaders; and ended the year by dominating the prestigious Macau Grand Prix at the wheel of a Formula Atlantic Ralt.

For 1980, Lees struggled manfully with the last two woefully uncompetitive F1 Shadows until the organisation ceased its racing activities in mid-season. Following an outing in the new F2 Ralt-Honda, Geoff committed himself to a full season with the team for 1981, and his press-on style of driving proved ideally suited for obtaining the championship laurels.

The reserved Lees had hoped that, by stepping back into F2 to win the championship rather than continue with uncompetitive teams in F1, his chances of attaining a decent Grand Prix drive would be enhanced, but this was not to be: with no sponsorship to his name, Lees's re-entry into F1 racing in 1982 failed to take place and his hopes of helping Honda's Grand Prix comeback were dashed when the company decided to entrust their F1 plans to Spirit and Stefan Johansson. In 1983, Geoff based himself in Japan, where he contested F2 and sportscar races for ex-F2 racer Tetsu Ikuzawa's JPS-sponsored team. Victory in his March-Honda at the final Suzaka round brought Geoff the country's F2 Championship title — the first man to secure both European and Japanese F2 honours.

Geoff Lees.

● **Corrado Fabi** comprises one half of the latest in a line of a motor racing phenomenon — racing driver brothers, he and his elder brother Teo forming the most successful racing driving fraternity since Pedro and Ricardo Rodriguez.

In fact, Corrado was the first of the two to take up karting, Teo's passion being skiing at the time. But, by 1976, both brothers were members of the European Championship-winning Italian National team — although Corrado's name was left off the cup as he was banned midway through the series for being under age! The first to be old enough to obtain a road licence, Teo's race driving career consequently leapt ahead of his brother's; he had already reached F2 by the time Corrado became 18 and could enter races at the wheel of Teo's old March F3 car. In 1980, Corrado contested the European F3 Championship in a Euroracing March, winning two races and only ceding the championship honours at the last round.

The following year, Teo — who had finished third for March in the European F2 Championship — travelled across the Atlantic to contest the CanAm sportscar series (before gaining an F1 seat at Toleman for 1982), and Corrado took over the vacant March seat to become the youngest

driver in the Formula, finishing fifth in the championship. 1982 proved to be one of the most closely-fought F2 seasons ever, but this time the smooth-driving 21-year-old took the honours for March by winning the all-important last race and four others. Next season brought a F1 drive with Osella, the fresh-faced Italian impressing on-lookers with his racecraft on the few occasions his mount qualified for Grands Prix. Teo, meanwhile, was consolidating his reputation in America as an outstanding rookie in the CART Indycar series, and rumours persisted that the talented brothers might eventually be united in a pukka March F1 team.

Corrado Fabi.

● **Jonathan Palmer**, the 1983 European Champion, is currently Britain's brightest motor racing prospect.

Eight years ago, when a young medical student, Palmer completed a trial drive at Brands Hatch Motor Racing Stables, and then drove modified GT and Formula Ford cars for a number of seasons whenever he could find the time between his hospital work and studies. Qualified as a doctor, Jonathan was able to embark on a full season of F3 in 1981, albeit on a shoestring budget. Although always a front runner in club racing, his results at the wheel of the West Surrey Engineering Ralt RT3 had remarkable impact, Jonathan winning the first four races in the Marlboro British F3 Championship and eventually becoming British F3 Champion with a total of eight wins and five second places to his credit.

This success led to a testing contract with the Williams F1 team and an offer from Ron Tauranac to campaign a Ralt-Honda in F2. In fact, 1982 turned out to be very much a learning season: the championship holders had pinned their faith on a new chassis, and it took Palmer a while to build up the knowledge and confidence needed to set the car up properly, whilst poor reliability meant that he only brought the Ralt home in the points on five occasions.

Jonathan determined to remain with the team for 1983 in the hope that the previous year's hard graft would be rewarded, and this was indeed what happened, a late-season charge bringing the combination five consecutive race wins and the championship title. The outcome was a testament to the calm, analytical and conscientious approach Jonathan brings to his driving, and to his dedication in seeking to continually improve the machinery at his disposal. At the end of the year, the new champion made his F1 début for Williams at the European Grand Prix, successfully qualifying his Cosworth-engined car and coolly and steadily steering it round Brands Hatch to finish 13th.

Jonathan Palmer.

9 The Classic Cars

Following on from the ultra-successful F2 Brabham-Honda, the BRABHAM BT23 was designed by Ron Tauranac as a straightforward single-seater space-frame chassis, easy to drive and maintain and therefore ideal for the privateer as well as the factory team. Powered by the 4-cylinder 16-valve Cosworth FVA engine, six cars appeared regularly during the course of the 1967 season, winning 11 of the 24 races in the hands of Jochen Rindt, Frank Gardner and Robin Widdows. The BT23C — incorporating minor suspension and steering improvements — followed in 1968 and,

although less reliable, proved popular with privateers, there being no works Brabham team in the Formula that year. Jochen Rindt cemented his reputation as 'King of F2' in his Winkelmann car, winning six races, while Jonathan Williams took Frank Williams's model to a victory at Monza. For 1969, Brabham produced a stiffer chassis, the BT30, but BT23C runners continued to enjoy some success, Robin Widdows and Brian Hart chalking up wins and Jacky Ickx showing strongly as a guest driver in Alistair Walker's car.

● The MATRA MS7 (also FVA-engined) first

Brabham-Cosworth BT23.

Matra-Cosworth MS7.

appeared during 1967 as a development of the scuttle-shaped MS5, Jackie Stewart winning three races in the Tyrell example and Jacky Ickx clinching the European Championship at Vallelunga in the same car. The works MS7 was less reliable, but in 1968 won three races in the hands of Jean-Pierre Beltoise (European Champion that year), while another victory was gained by team-mate Henri Pescarolo, who followed Beltoise home on two occasions. Ken Tyrell's F2 programme was affected by Jackie Stewart's wrist injury at Jarama, although the Scotsman managed three wins from his four starts. With its immensely rigid monocoque and clean bodyshape, the MS7 handled well, was rapid and reliable to boot, and was hardly developed throughout its racing life as Matra were too busy with their F1 projects. In 1969, Stewart took three more victories, while Beltoise, Pescarolo and Johnny Servoz-Gavin (in the second Tyrell MS7) won one race apiece — the latter becoming Matra's third consecutive European Champion. New fuel tank regulations rendered the MS7 ineligible for competition the following season, and so Matra's involvement in the category ended.

● Having signed an exclusive contract to use BMW's four-cylinder single-plug head 16-valve engine for 1973, March developed a chassis and tyres round it, producing a compact, snub-nosed car with high cockpit surround. The MARCH 732 dominated the Formula, its braking capabilities and the BMW engine's torque being particularly impressive, and Jean-Pierre Jarier swept to the European Championship with eight race wins for the works. March were gaining an increasing

share of the F2 customer market, and the success of the 732 brought further buyers in mid-season: Vittorio Brambilla won two races in his Beta-sponsored car, while Roger Williamson (Wheat-croft Racing) and Jacques Coulon (Brian Lewis) took a victory each. That the success of the 732 — designed by Harvey Postlethwaite and Robin Herd — wasn't entirely due to its engine was proved in Formula Atlantic, where, using BDA power, the same chassis was virtually unbeatable. Although the factory cars for 1974 proved very different from the 732, the 742s supplied to March customers were little more than updated specifications of the previous year's model: the only one to interrupt another year of works domination was the BP France car (rebodied by Tico Martini) of Jacques Laffite, who won at Salzburg.

● After a period of being beaten by French cars using the Renault V6 race engine, March and BMW decided to come up with an entirely new design with which to establish their supremacy in the wake of the French teams' withdrawal from F2 in 1978. While BMW concentrated on obtaining more horsepower from the faithful M12 four cylinder, the MARCH 782 (designed by Robin Herd) involved an entire re-think on weight distribution, with the driver sitting further forward in the monocoque than usual and the water radiator moved from the side to the nose. Works driver Bruno Giacomelli went on to win eight of the 12 races (and the European Championship), with team-mate Marc Surer runner-up on five occasions. Impressive testing performances well before the season began brought plenty of customer orders, and several privateers finished in the points alongside the five works entries. Brian

March-BMW 732.

March-BMW 782.

Henton and Alex Ribeiro proved the 782 could run competitively with Hart power behind it, while Piero Necchi showed the chassis was well-suited to Pirelli radials as well as the standard Goodyear tyres. The advent of 'ground-effect' outdated the 782 specification as a development vehicle for 1979, although the Toleman Group drivers reverted to them on occasions, Rad Dougall winning at Thruxton and Brian Henton finishing second at the Nürburgring.

● The TOLEMAN TG280 was designed by Rory Byrne following the Toleman Group's development of the previous year's Ralt. A tidy, conventional ground-effect car, powered by the Hart 420R engine, the TG280 incorporated a low-slung driver's seat which enabled the sidepods to touch the ground under load, thereby creating a partial vacuum as sliding skirts (banned in F2 for 1980) would have done previously. Contracted to Pirelli, who were keen to establish a competitive range of

Toleman-Hart TG280.

race tyres, Toleman based their development work around the Italian radials, the car running better on stiffer shoulders. The B specification TG280, which appeared in mid-season, improved straight-line speed and increased downforce by moving the rear suspension above the gearbox and out of the venturi system underneath the car. The Toleman proved a winner from the word go, Brian Henton finally claiming the European Championship with three wins to his credit, and fellow works driver Derek Warwick finishing runner up with a win at Silverstone and a couple of results behind his team-mate. Three customer cars were sold, and Siegfried Stohr and Huub Rothengatter managed a win apiece. The following season, their sights on F1, Toleman arranged for Lola to build TG280 replicas and entrusted Docking-Spitzley to run the main effort: Stefan Johansson won two races (at the start and end of the season), but further success eluded the team as Pirelli moved away from stiff sidewall tyres. For 1982, the cars featured revised suspension and new aerodynamics: after nearly finishing 1–2 in the opening wet race, the Tolemans suffered from lack of development due to the financial constraints upon the team and a number of serious accidents.

● Although used to building construction chassis, the RALT RH6H was designed by Ron Tauranac as an out-and-out purpose-built race winner, using honeycomb technology. Attached to the 325bhp Honda V6 engine, the cars were hurriedly produced and were disappointing in 1982, suffering from varying feedback from the comparatively inexperienced drivers, tyre wear problems and a spate of high-speed accidents. However, in 1983, with Mike Thackwell back in the team and Jonathan Palmer retained from the

Ralt-Honda RH6H/83.

previous season, the RH6H finally came good. The chassis now featured pull-rod front suspension, a wider front track and more efficient aerodynamics, while Honda now drew 340bhp from their motor. Tauranac opted for the more consistent Michelin tyres this year, and the cars benefited from the pre-season testing denied them in 1982. Palmer won at Hockenheim early in the season, and the RH6H/83s proved exceptionally reliable, but it wasn't until mid-season, when further attention had been given to the cars' weight and suspension, that they became consistent race leaders. Following a victory for Thackwell at Jarama, Jonathan Palmer put on an unequalled series of performances, winning five consecutive races (two of them 1–2s with Thackwell) to claim the European Championship and help Ralt-Honda to the new F2 Constructor's Cup.

Acknowledgements

I am indebted to a number of people for their assistance whilst I was writing this book. In particular, I would like to thank Judy Holland for her advice on publishing; Quentin Spurring and Mark Hughes for granting me research facilities at *Autosport* and access to photographs; *Motor Sport* for similar help, and Kathy Ager for guiding my way through the extensive archives of the magazine's photographic unit, LAT; Barry Bland, of the Formula Two Association; Ian Phillips; Dave Scott, for giving me his time in the middle of a highly strenuous racing season; Jacques de la Beraudière and François Guiter, of Elf Oil; Jonathan Palmer for contributing the Foreword; and my mother, José Wood, who typed the final manuscript. Special thanks to Sally Phillips for her encouragement, her tolerance, her travelling companionship — and her Italian!

Tristan Wood
Spring, 1984

Photo Credits: LAT pages 6, 9, 10, 15–20, 27–37, 42–45, 48, 50, 54 (bottom), 56–59, 64, 66 (bottom), 73, 74, 76 (bottom), 77 (top), 79 (bottom), 80, 81 (top), 82, 87, 101, 109, 110, 113, 114 (right), 117, 118 (right), 119, 120, 121 (right), 122–125; *Autosport* pages 11, 14, 22, 23, 25, 26, 39, 41, 46, 47, 51, 52, 54 (top), 61–63, 71, 77 (bottom), 111, 112, 114 (left), 115, 116, 121 (left), 126 (top); National Motor Museum, Beaulieu, page 8; Peter Bell page 24; Ford of Germany page 79 (top); BMW page 81 (bottom); BP Oil page 85; Elf Oil pages 86 (bottom), 118 (left); Sally Phillips rear cover inset. All remaining photos and circuit diagrams by the author.